GENIUS

GREAT INVENTORS AND THEIR CREATIONS

JACK CHALLONER

CARLTON

CONTENTS

RIGHT:
Palaeolithic arrow head. The history of technology begins with unknown "geniuses" fashioning tools and weapons from stone.

THIS IS A CARLTON BOOK

A previous edition of this title was published in 2010.

This new edition published in 2013 by Carlton Books Ltd, a division of the Carlton Publishing Group, 20 Mortimer Street, London W1T 3JW

Text © Jack Challoner 2010
Design © Carlton Books Ltd 2010, 2013

Produced under licence from SCMG Enterprises Ltd, Science Museum ® SCMG. Every purchase supports the museum. www.sciencemuseum.org.uk

The Science Museum is the most popular destination for science, technology and engineering in the UK. Offering visitors of all ages an incredible collection of objects, both historical and cutting edge, as well as contemporary science learning and debate, we help make sense of the science that shapes our lives and gives inspiration to scientists of the future.

A CIP catalogue record for this book is available from the British Library.

ISBN 978 1 78097 365 4

Printed in China

INTRODUCTION

THIS BOOK IS A CELEBRATION OF SOME OF THE PEOPLE WHOSE BRILLIANT MINDS AND PERSEVERANCE HAVE HELPED SHAPE THE MODERN WORLD. THEY ARE BY NO MEANS THE ONLY GENIUSES IN HISTORY, NOR ARE THEY THE ONLY GREAT INVENTORS. BUT THE 28 PEOPLE WHOSE BIOGRAPHIES FEATURE IN THIS BOOK ARE ICONS IN THE HISTORY OF TECHNOLOGY.

Genius: Great Inventors and their Inventions is organized chronologically by the birth dates of the inventors, beginning with Archimedes of Syracuse (born c. 287 BCE). Of course, the history of technology does not begin with Archimedes. You can trace its beginnings back to the first stone tools fashioned by our distant ancestors in Africa more than two million years ago. More recently, old stone age (Palaeolithic) people invented weaponry, fire-making and clothing; and around eleven thousand years ago, new stone age (Neolithic) people in the Fertile Crescent, in Mesopotamia and the Levant, began farming and building houses. The great civilizations that followed in ancient Mesopotamia, China, India and Egypt – introduced many fundamental technologies. Innovations such as the wheel, bricks, boats, ploughs and the smelting of metals are still of great importance today, but in most cases, little or nothing is known of the inventors' lives.

After Archimedes, we note the great contribution by early Islamic scholars to the history of science and technology by featuring the Arab engineer al-Jazarī, before moving on to Renaissance Europe, where the seeds of the modern world were sown. In the 1440s, Johannes Gutenberg brought together a number of existing technologies to invent the printing press, which quickly spread new ideas and encouraged literacy. Renaissance polymath Leonardo da Vinci's technological genius was perhaps too far ahead of its time, and as a result, he had less influence on the development of technology than he could have had. Scientific instruments such as the telescope, the microscope and the thermometer, invented in the sixteenth century (see Hans Lipperhey and Cornelius Drebbel), were crucial in the "Scientific Revolution" that gave people a desire, and the means, to understand of the world. As science matured, it began to play an increasingly important role in the process of invention (see Benjamin Franklin).

Science was also important in the Industrial Revolution, which began in Britain in the 1750s. It helped usher in a "mechanistic" view of the world, which helped advance engineering and contributed to the development of the steam engine (see James Watt). High-pressure steam (see Richard Trevithick) went on to power railway locomotives, bringing about a revolution in transport. Discoveries in physics, chemistry and biology underpinned most of the other important advances of the nineteenth century, including the electric motor and generator (see Michael Faraday), photography (see Nicephore Niépce), and antiseptic surgery (see Joseph Lister). Many of the inventions that characterize the modern world were developed between 1870 and 1930, including the telephone, the motor car, electrification, television, radio, sound recording, cinema, the aeroplane, the helicopter and artificial fertilizers. Nearly half the inventors featured in this book were active in that period, which historians often refer to as the "Second Industrial Revolution". But innovation has not faltered since then: the second half of the twentieth century saw rockets reach the Moon (see Wernher von Braun), the rise of electronic computers (see Alan Turing), tremendous advances in medicine (see Gertrude Elion) and the invention of the World Wide Web (see Tim Berners-Lee).

Nearly all the people featured in this book are white men. It is certainly not the case that women or non-Caucasians are not inventive, not clever or not important. It is simply the case that during those first and second Industrial Revolutions, the most important technological advances occurred in rich, industrialized countries which, at the time, were in Europe and North America. In the societies that existed in these countries at the time, those people privileged with education and opportunity - and recognized for their achievements – were mostly white men. Today, things are very different – although there is still a long way to go before everyone everywhere has similar opportunities to become a genius who can change the world.

RIGHT: *A modern "arrow head", a pointer from a computer display, illustrates how much the world has changed, thanks to human ingenuity.*

ARCHIMEDES

(c.287 BCE–c.212 BCE)

THE GREATEST AND BEST-KNOWN INVENTOR OF THE ANCIENT WORLD WAS ALSO ONE OF ITS GREATEST MATHEMATICIANS: ARCHIMEDES OF SYRACUSE. A GREAT DEAL IS KNOWN ABOUT HIS MATHEMATICAL ACHIEVEMENTS FROM HIS OWN WRITINGS, BUT ANY KNOWLEDGE OF HIS REMARKABLE INVENTIONS EXISTS ONLY BECAUSE HIS CONTEMPORARIES DOCUMENTED THEM.

Archimedes was born in Syracuse, on the island of Sicily, then a colony of the Grecian Empire. Little is known about his life or what kind of person he was. The little that is known comes from commentaries written by historians who lived at the time or over the next hundred or so years. The most important source is Greek-born Greek and Roman biographer and historian Plutarch (c.46–120 CE).

According to Plutarch, Archimedes's father was an astronomer and the family was closely related to the ruler of Syracuse, King Hiero (also spelled Hieron) II (c.306–215 BCE). The king's reign endured almost as long as Archimedes's entire life – and many of Archimedes's activities were connected to Hiero.

King Hiero asked Archimedes to design a pump to drain his ship during the voyage to Alexandria, Egypt. Archimedes devised a simple but brilliant solution. The device, today known as the Archimedes Screw (or Archimedean Screw) consists of a helical blade – a wide screw thread – inside a cylinder. The screw lifts water when it turns, and was so effective that it was quickly adopted

ABOVE: *The* Archimedes Palimpsest – *a book of Christian prayers (horizontal) written in the twelfth century over a tenth-century copy of some of Archimedes's most important works (vertical). Scientists at the Walters Art Museum in Baltmore, USA, have used a variety of techniques to make the Archimedes text more visible.*

BELOW: *An 1815 print showing the inside of an Archimedes Screw, normally housed in a cylinder. Turning the handle clockwise drags the water up the screw thread, through the cylinder, so that it emerges at the top. The device was used extensively for irrigation in Archimedes's day, and brought him great fame.*

in many countries for irrigation. Archimedean Screws remain commonplace today in factories and on earth-moving machines, where they are used to move granular materials such as soil and plastic pellets. They are also still in use for irrigation worldwide.

Archimedes brought together mathematics and experimental and mechanical principles, and clearly realized the close and important connection between them. He studied the mathematics of the day – in Alexandria – and quickly moved beyond it. It is his exquisite mathematical proofs and inspired ideas that reveal his true genius.

Although none of Archimedes's original work in his own hand exists, there are several copies made during the first thousand or so years after his death. The most important is an eleventh-century manuscript on vellum. Archimedes's work had been scraped off, overwritten with Christian prayers, and bound together as part of a book. Since this book, now called the *Archimedes Palimpsest*, was bought at auction in 1998, scientists have been applying the latest imaging techniques to try to "see through" the Christian text

to enable them to read Archimedes's work for the first time. One of the most remarkable findings from the analysis of this book is that Archimedes invented some of the principles of the mathematical technique today called calculus. Crucial to modern science and technology, calculus was only actually formalized in the late seventeenth century, by Isaac Newton (1643–1727) and Gottfried Leibniz (1646–1716).

Archimedes used what would today be called applied mathematics, calculating the centres of gravity of various objects and working out the mathematics behind "simple machines" such as levers, pulleys and gears.

He used his knowledge of gears to invent a small, wheeled cart that could measure long distances (an odometer), a clock that struck the hours, and devices to predict the positions of the sun, the moon and the five planets that were then known. In 1900, divers discovered what scholars deduced was an ancient astronomical computer in a wreck off the coast of the Greek island Antikythera. Some historians believe that this computer may be closely descended from the work of Archimedes.

Of all Archimedes's inventions, the ones most celebrated in his lifetime were the weapons he designed to defend Syracuse during the siege of the city by the Romans, which began in 214 BCE. The weapons included the Claw – a crane fixed to the city wall that could lift Roman ships out of the water and drop or capsize them.

BLOCK AND TACKLE

Ancient civilizations made use of what physicists call "simple machines": the lever, the ramp, the wheel and axle; the inclined plane, the wedge and the pulley. Archimedes was almost certainly the first to combine two pulleys, to make a device that could exert a huge force. That device, the block and tackle, is still used today for lifting or pulling heavy loads.

According to Plutarch, Archimedes invented the block and tackle in response to a challenge set by King Hiero after Archimedes had suggested that there is no weight too great to be moved by a lever. Hiero challenged Archimedes to move the huge and heavy ship *Syracusia*, a feat normally only achieved by teams of many strong men. Archimedes single-handedly moved the ship, complete with crew and cargo, not with a lever but with a block and tackle.

ABOVE: Part of the Antikythera mechanism, which appears to be an ancient astronomical calculator and was recovered from the wreck of a Roman ship dating to the first century BCE. Archimedes is known to have built devices for this purpose and many academics believe this could be one of them.

RIGHT: An ancient Roman mosaic depicting the death of Archimedes. The mosaic was uncovered early in the nineteenth century during French excavations of Pompeii, Italy. It shows Archimedes at his table with an abacus – and a Roman soldier apparently telling Archimedes to leave the room.

AL-JAZARĪ
(1136–1206)

MOST PEOPLE ARE AWARE OF THE TREMENDOUS SCIENTIFIC AND TECHNOLOGICAL ADVANCES OF THE GREAT ANCIENT CIVILIZATIONS IN EGYPT, CHINA, INDIA, GREECE AND ROME. BUT DURING THE MIDDLE AGES, THE ISLAMIC EMPIRE KEPT THE SPIRIT OF LEARNING AND INNOVATION ALIVE. ONE OF ITS GREATEST TECHNICAL GENIUSES WAS A MECHANICAL ENGINEER NAMED AL-JAZARĪ.

Badi' al-Zaman Abu al-'Izz Isma'il ibn al-Razzaz al-Jazarī was born in an area of Mesopotamia called al-Jazira, in what is now part of modern-day southern Turkey. Al-Jazarī lived at the height of the Islamic Golden Age, also sometimes called the Islamic Renaissance. The spread of Islam in the seventh century had encouraged a rich culture and a stable political system – the Caliphate. By 750 CE, the Caliphate covered a huge area, from northern Spain in the west, through the Middle East and North Africa, to the fringes of China in the east. Throughout this Islamic Empire, there was a great emphasis on learning; scholars collected and translated all the knowledge they could from around the world and added their own. From the ninth to the twelfth century, the Caliphate

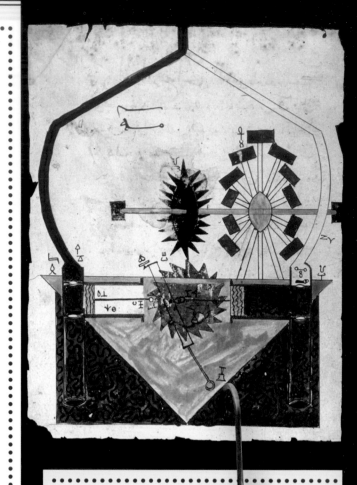

ABOVE RIGHT: *Water-raising pump from al-Jazarī's* Book of Knowledge of Mechanical Devices. *Pistons driven by a water wheel open and close valves, drawing water from the river (blue) and pushing it up through the two pipes, which join to form a single pipe (top).*

THE INFLUENCE OF ISLAMIC SCHOLARS

During the Islamic Golden Age, the centre of scholarly activity was the House of Wisdom in Baghdad (in modern Iraq). Both a library and a centre for translation, the House of Wisdom acted not only as a repository for the books and ideas of ancient thinkers from Greece and China, but also as a centre of excellence for contemporary scholars.

Much of the knowledge collected, translated and expanded by medieval Islamic scholars passed into Europe in the twelfth and thirteenth centuries. A dedicated band of European scholars sought out works in Spain and Sicily after these areas came under Christian rule. They translated what they found into Latin, and the resulting documents formed the basis of early scientific study in Europe.

The works of the Islamic scientists, mathematicians, astronomers and doctors contained significant advances in fields such as atomic theory, optics, surgery, chemistry and mathematics. Kept alive in the universities of medieval Europe, their ideas inspired the Scientific Revolution of the sixteenth and seventeenth centuries.

AVICENNA
ex codice antiquo Galeni

ABOVE: *Model of pump shown above, built for a 1976 exhibition called "Science and Technology in Islam" at the Science Museum, London, part of the countrywide Festival of Islam. The mechanisms are mostly hidden; most prominent is the waterwheel that would have driven the device.*

LEFT: *Persian scholar Abu Ali Ibn Sina, better known by his Latinized name Avicenna (c.980–1037 AD). Avicenna was a key figure in the transmission of classical Greek and Roman ideas to medieval Europe, but also contributed many of his own ideas and experiences, in more than 200 books.*

was the foremost intellectual centre of the world.

Out of the stability and the learning came great wealth, and powerful dynasties ruled over each region. Al-Jazarī became chief engineer to the Artuqid dynasty in the town of Diyar Bakir, after his father retired from the same position in 1174. Most of what we know about al-Jazarī comes from a book he completed shortly before his death. The *Kitáb fí ma'rifat al-hiyal al-handasiyya* (*Book of Knowledge of Mechanical Devices*) is a compendium of the engineering designs he created through his career. According to the book's introduction, Nasir al-Din Mahmud ibn Muhammad, the dynasty's ruler between 1200 and 1222, commissioned al-Jazarī to write the book in 1198. Al-Jazarī's book contains details of 50 ingenious devices, including intricate clocks, fountains that regularly change their flow patterns, machines for raising water and toys for entertainment. The description of each device is accompanied by clear drawings that help explain how it was constructed and how it worked.

The spread of Islam brought huge advances in science, mathematics, medicine and philosophy. Engineering, on the other hand – although held in great esteem and practised competently – was mostly just a continuation of existing technologies established by the Greeks and the Romans. There were certainly notable exceptions, and some of those innovations are to be found in al-Jazarī's wonderful book. For example, al-Jazarī's water- or donkey-powered devices made use of power-transmission elements that had been used for centuries: gears, levers and pulleys. But in one of his inventions, a double-acting piston pump, he gives the first known reference to a crankshaft – a device for changing rotary motion to back-and-forth motion (or vice versa). He also makes extensive use of the camshaft, a rotating cylinder with pegs protruding from it; his is the first mention of that, too. Al-Jazar also invented the first known combination lock and the earliest known mechanical water-supply system, which was installed in Damascus in the thirteenth century, to supply hospitals and mosques across the city.

Several of al-Jazarī's contraptions featured automata: animal or human figures that made precise, programmed movements. For example, he describes a boat containing four automated musicians that entertained at parties and an automated girl figure that refilled a wash basin. Automatons also feature in most of al-Jazarī's clocks, which were more elaborate and ingenious than any that had come before. Most impressive was his "castle clock". More than 3 metres (10 feet) high, it displayed the constellations of the zodiac, with the orbits of the Sun and the Moon, and doors that opened every hour to reveal papier-mâché figures. This extraordinary device could also be programmed to take account of the varying day lengths.

LEFT: *Model of a blood-letting device described in al-Jazarī's* Book of Knowledge of Mechanical Devices. *Blood-letting (phlebotomy) was a popular practice in medieval Islamic medicine. This device measured the volume of blood lost during blood-letting sessions.*

ABOVE: *Glass alembic, approximately eleventh century. An alembic is an essential tool in distillation, a procedure for purifying mixtures. Distillation was pioneered by Islamic chemists, who developed many processes that would later be important in the development of the science of chemistry.*

LEFT: *Reconstruction of al-Jazarī's elephant clock at the Ibn Battuta Mall in Dubai, United Arab Emirates. Every half-hour, the scribe on the elephant's back rotates full circle, and at the end of each half-hour, the figure of the mahout (elephant driver) beats a drum and a cymbal sounds.*

JOHANNES GUTENBERG

(c.1400–3 FEBRUARY 1468)

I
T IS DIFFICULT TO OVERESTIMATE
THE IMPORTANCE OF THE PRINTING
PRESS IN THE HISTORY OF THE WORLD.
THE MASS-PRODUCTION
OF BOOKS MADE THEM
CHEAPER AND MORE
ACCESSIBLE, WHICH
PROMOTED LITERACY AND
THE SPREAD OF IDEAS.
THE CREATOR OF THIS
INFLUENTIAL NEW TECHNOLOGY
WAS A GERMAN GOLDSMITH
NAMED JOHANNES GUTENBERG.

Little is known of the early life of
Johannes (or Johann) Gutenberg. It is known that
he was born in Mainz, Germany, around 1400, and that he came
from the privileged, governing elite. He attended university, where he
would have come into contact with books, and he trained as a goldsmith.

Around 1420, several families were exiled from Mainz after a rebellion
by the tax-paying middle class. Gutenberg's was among them, and he
travelled to Strasbourg, where he was involved in several ventures. One of
them, he told his financial backers, was "a secret". It is very likely that this
secret was the development of the printing press.

At the time, nearly all books were painstakingly written out by
scribes. Books, therefore, were rare and extremely expensive, and literacy
was confined to religious and political leaders. Woodblock printing
produced a few books – but each block, representing a whole page, had
to be carved in its entirety. Gutenberg's important innovation, "moveable
type", changed all that.

Moveable type is a system of printing in which a page of text is
arranged in a frame, or matrix, by slotting in individual raised letters. The
letters are then inked and pressed onto paper. It was invented in Korea and
in China in the eleventh century, but never caught on, mostly because of
the large number of characters that are used in written Chinese and Korean.

Gutenberg invented moveable type independently, and his approach
was simple and efficient. First, he carefully made punches of hardened steel,
each with the raised shape of a letter. With these, he punched impressions
of the letters into copper. Next, he fitted the "negative"

ABOVE LEFT: *Portrait of Johannes Gutenberg, 1584.
Gutenberg's printing press made it possible to mass-
produce books, enabling the rapid spread of new ideas. His
most important invention was the hand mould, in which
he cast copies of individual letters from an alloy of lead,
tin and antimony.*

RIGHT: *Coloured nineteenth-century artist's impression
of a scene in Gutenberg's workshop (artist unknown).
Gutenberg, bearded, is shown in the foreground, checking
a printed page. There would actually have been about 20
people working in the workshop at any one time.*

BELOW: *The frontispiece of the oldest dated printed
book. Bought from the monk in a cave in Dunhuang,
China in 1907, this copy of the Buddhist text
Diamond Sutra is on a scroll 5 metres (16 feet)
long. It was printed using woodblocks in 868 CE.*

BELOW: *A type case filled with
large, decorative moveable type in a reconstruction
of Gutenberg's printing workshop at the Gutenberg
Museum in Mainz, Germany. A printer would
slot these individual pieces of type into a frame, to
represent the text of one page of a book.*

copper pieces into a hand-held mould of his own invention, and poured in molten metal to cast as many perfect copies of the letters as he needed. The metal Gutenberg used was an alloy of lead, tin and antimony that has a low melting point and solidified quickly inside the mould. His alloy is still used wherever "founder's type" or "hot metal" letterpress printing methods survive today.

While still in Strasbourg in the 1440s, Gutenberg experimented with another crucial element of his printing system: the press. Gutenberg's press was adapted from winemakers' screw presses. The inked, typeset text was slotted face-up on a flat bed, covered with paper, then slid underneath a heavy stone; turning the screw then pressed the paper onto the type. Repeating the process gave exact copies time after time. Gutenberg also formulated oil-based ink, which was more durable than the water-based inks in use at the time. He knew that by putting all these technologies together he was onto something very important.

By 1448, Gutenberg was back in Mainz. He borrowed money from a wealthy investor, Johann Fust (c.1400–1466), to set up a printing shop there. Knowing that the church would be the main source of business, Gutenberg decided to print bibles. Work on the Gutenberg Bible began around 1452, after several test prints of other works, including books on Latin grammar. The relatively low price of the bibles, and their exquisite quality, secured the success of Gutenberg's new technology, which then spread quickly across Europe. By 1500, millions of books had been printed. Gutenberg had created the first media revolution.

LEFT: *A highly decorated page from a Gutenberg Bible. Gutenberg produced 180 copies of his bible. Some were on vellum, others on paper; some were decorated (by hand), others were left plain. The books caused a sensation when they were first displayed at a trade fair in Frankfurt in 1454.*

BELOW LEFT: *Portrait of German playwright Aloys Senefelder, the inventor of lithography. His process enabled printing of illustrations from a flat surface; artists could draw directly onto it, using special water-repellent inks.*

Unfortunately for Gutenberg, Johann Fust demanded his money back, and accused Gutenberg of embezzlement. A judge ordered Gutenberg to hand over his printing equipment as payment. Fust went on to become a successful printer, and Gutenberg set up a smaller printing shop in the nearby city of Bamberg. Gutenberg later moved to a small village where, in 1465, he was finally recognized for his invention and given an annual pension. He died three years later in relative poverty.

ROTARY PRINTING PRESS

Although Gutenberg's invention dramatically changed the course of history in a very short time, printing was still a painstaking process. It required several people and produced only a hundred or so sheets per hour. The invention of cast-iron presses and the introduction of steam power in the nineteenth century improved that rate to about a thousand pages an hour. A further major step in the history of printing was the invention of the rotary press in 1843, by American inventor Richard March Hoe (1812–1886).

Hoe's steam-powered invention could print millions of pages per day, largely due to the fact that paper could be fed in through rollers as a continuous sheet. Hoe's device relied upon lithography, a process invented by Bavarian author Aloys Senefelder (1771–1834). In lithography, ink is applied to smooth surfaces rather than to raised type, which was ideally suited to the drum of Hoe's press.

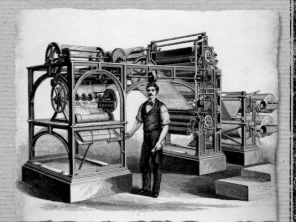

LEONARDO DA VINCI
(15 APRIL 1452–2 MAY 1519)

THE NAME LEONARDO DA VINCI IS SYNONYMOUS WITH GENIUS, YET ARGUABLY THE ITALIAN POLYMATH DOES NOT BELONG IN THIS BOOK. ALTHOUGH HE WAS UNDOUBTEDLY A GENIUS, AND HE CERTAINLY CHANGED THE WORLD, HIS INFLUENCE ON HISTORY WAS LARGELY RESTRICTED TO DEVELOPMENTS IN ART. HIS SCIENTIFIC RESEARCHES WERE NOT WELL KNOWN IN HIS LIFETIME, AND MOST OF HIS INVENTIONS WERE NEVER BUILT.

Leonardo da Vinci was the archetypal Renaissance man. He had an enormous influence on the development of painting, drawing and sculpture. He was a pioneer of perspective and of using anatomical studies to improve life drawing; he was an innovator in how to paint light and shade, in using new materials and in composition. That Leonardo was also a great scientist, engineer and inventor only became common knowledge when his journals were published long after his death.

Leonardo was born in Vinci, a town in Tuscany, Italy. His father was a local notary, and his mother a peasant. At the age of sixteen, he became an apprentice at the workshop of artist Andrea del Verrocchio (c.1435–1488) in Florence, where his talents shone through. He qualified as a master at the age of 20, and worked in Florence, then in Milan, where he created such iconic paintings as *The Adoration of the Magi*, *The Virgin of the Rocks* and *The Last Supper*.

Throughout his life, and particularly during his time in Milan, Leonardo kept detailed notebooks. There were an estimated 13,000 pages in all, containing his observations, thoughts, sketches and inventions. Around 5,000 of these pages survive today.

The notebooks reveal how Leonardo followed the scientific method – based on careful observation, scepticism and experiment – well before the likes of Galileo Galilei (1564–1642) and Isaac Newton (1643–1727). Leonardo's grasp of optics, geology, hydrodynamics (the behaviour of water), astronomy and the principles behind gears, levers, cantilevers and force and motion was far ahead of his time.

Leonardo had a chance to apply some of his knowledge and

LEFT: *Self portrait c.1510. Leonardo's supreme draughtsmanship was in part due to his hands-on experience of anatomy.*

BELOW: *Model of a revolving crane. Leonardo's twin cranes were designed for quarrying. Stones cut from a rock face would be loaded into one bucket; the whole crane would then rotate, and the bucket would be emptied while another was loaded.*

ABOVE: *Model based on Leonardo's design for a screw-cutting machine. Turning the crank handle causes the dowel in the centre to turn. At the same time, it turns the two side screws, advancing the cutting tool along the length of the wooden dowel in the centre.*

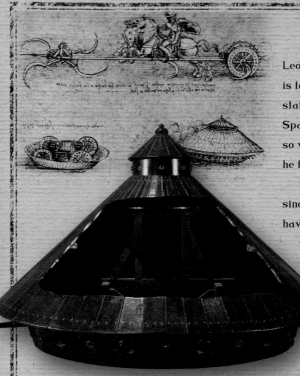

LEONARDO'S MILITARY INVENTIONS

Leonardo da Vinci lived during a turbulent time in Italy's history. In fact, Italy as it is today did not then exist, but was largely a collection of frequently warring city states. In addition, there were constant threats from, and takeovers by, the French and Spanish. Rich patrons would do anything to protect their wealth, status and territories, so when Leonardo suggested he could build terrifying weapons and defence systems, he found willing supporters.

It is ironic that Leonardo should have produced such terrifying, warlike designs, since he was a committed pacifist. Perhaps that is why, in some cases, he seems to have introduced flaws into the designs deliberately, or withheld crucial information, which would prevent them from working. One pertinent example is his design for a tank, sketched out in detail more than four hundred years before any tanks were constructed. Leonardo's tank was to be powered by eight men turning cranks. When the design was built for a television series in 2004, it would not move until one of the gears was reversed, a basic error that was probably intentional, rather than an oversight.

understanding when he worked as an engineer and military architect for two dukes of Milan from 1485 until 1499, and afterwards in the same capacity for other patrons, including the infamous Cesare Borgia (1475–1507). Indeed, when Leonardo was offering his services to these men, he made a point of promising them wonderful engineering projects, and only mentioned in passing that he was also a painter.

Among Leonardo's notebooks were detailed plans for many incredible inventions, most of which were almost certainly never built. These included a huge crossbow, various flying machines, a parachute, an armoured vehicle, a dredging machine, a helicopter, a humanoid mechanical robot, an aqualung, a bicycle and a water-powered alarm clock.

Since the nineteenth century, there has been great interest in Leonardo among academics and the general public alike. In recent years, several of his inventions that had only ever existed on paper have at last been constructed. Leonardo's designs have been found to work remarkably well, albeit with a bit of adaptation in some cases.

A few of Leonardo's inventions did make it out of his notebooks in his day, and were used by other people, but because there was no patent system in Italy at the time, there is little record of exactly which inventions passed into general use, or how. Two known examples are a bobbin-winding machine and a lens-grinding machine. Ingenious though they are, these devices do not do justice to Leonardo's enormous genius and foresight.

In 1513, Leonardo met the king of France, Francis I (1494–1547), after the king's conquest of Milan. Francis commissioned Leonardo to make him an automaton in the form of a lion. Leonardo made one that walked, turned its head and even presented a bunch of orchids when stroked in the right way. Francis was so impressed that he became Leonardo's patron, and Leonardo lived out his last three years of life in Amboise, France. There he died peacefully, renowned for his astonishing artistic skill but almost unknown for his scientific insight and his remarkable inventions.

ABOVE LEFT: *Leonardo's assault tank – a model built by IBM and on display at Château du Clos Lucé, France, Leonardo's final home. The shell of this hand-cranked tank was reinforced with metal plates containing holes so that the soldiers could fire weapons from within. Behind can be seen the sketches he made and on which the model was based*

BELOW: *Model of Leonardo's car. Leonardo intended it to be powered by spring-driven clockwork. It has no driver's seat, because this was designed to be an automaton. Like most of Leonardo's remarkable inventions, the car was not built in his lifetime.*

HANS LIPPERHEY
(1570 – September 1619)

THE TELESCOPE HAS ENABLED US TO DISCOVER OUR PLACE IN THE UNIVERSE, AND TO REVEAL THE TREASURES AND SHEER SCALE OF DEEP SPACE. NOBODY IS REALLY SURE WHO WAS THE FIRST TO CONSTRUCT A PRACTICAL TELESCOPE OR WHOSE GENIUS WAS THE FIRST TO REALIZE THE POTENTIAL FOR THIS DEVICE. BUT DUTCH LENS MAKER HANS LIPPERHEY WAS THE FIRST TO APPLY FOR A PATENT, IN 1608.

Hans Lipperhey (sometimes spelled Lippershey) was born in Wesel, Germany, and moved to Middelburg, in the Netherlands (then the Dutch Republic), in 1594. In the same year he married, became a Dutch citizen and opened a spectacle shop in the city. Little is known of his life, but what is clear is that he was the first person to apply for a patent for the telescope, which was called a "*kijker*" (Dutch for "viewer").

In September 1608, Lipperhey travelled to The Hague, the political centre of the Dutch Republic, where he filed the patent application for his device. His application was denied, because of the simplicity of the invention – it was really just two lenses held at a certain distance apart in a tube. However, the officials at The Hague saw the potential of Lipperhey's instrument, and commissioned him to build three sets of double-telescopes (i.e. binoculars). The Dutch States General paid Lipperhey handsomely for his work: he received more than enough to buy the house next to his and pay to have major renovation work carried out.

BELOW: Artist's impression of Hans Lipperhey in his workshop, experimenting with lenses during his invention of the telescope. The eyepiece lens magnifies the image produced by the larger, objective lens. The lens grinding machines and lathes are powered by treadles beneath the benches.

LEFT: Lens grinding machine, designed by Leonardo da Vinci. Lipperhey would have used a machine like this to grind concave lenses for the eyepieces of his telescopes and a slightly different machine to make the larger, convex lens that collects the light (the objective lens).

RIGHT: Compound microscope designed by English scientist Robert Hooke (1635-1703), whose 1665 book Micrographia *revealed the microscopic world to the public for the first time. Unfortunately, Lipperhey died long before the book was published. The glass balls and lenses focused light onto the specimen.*

GALILEO GALILEI
(1564–1542)

Although Lipperhey was by all accounts a gifted craftsman, and was the first to submit a patent application for the telescope, Galileo is the real genius in this story. His careful and thorough observation of the moon and his discovery and observations of the moons of Jupiter were key in overturning the longstanding, dogmatic theory that the earth is at the centre of the Universe.

Galileo improved the basic telescope design, and by August 1609, had managed to make his own instrument with a magnification of 8x (8-to-1), compared to Lipperhey's instrument, which could only magnify 3x. In the 1610s, he also experimented with the compound microscope, and in the 1620s, he became one of the first to make biological observations with microscopes.

Galileo was a great thinker, and is often called the father of physics or even the father of modern science. He was much more a pure scientist than an inventor, although he did invent a primitive thermometer and a geometrical compass, and he did not actually invent the telescope.

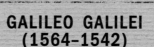

As it turns out, the States General was probably justified in refusing Lipperhey a patent. Within a few weeks, another Dutch spectacle maker, Jacob Metius (1571–1630), submitted a very similar application. In the 1620s, yet another retrospective claim for primacy of the invention of the telescope came to light. Zacharius Janssen (1580–1638), whose house was a few doors away from Lipperhey's, may have beaten Lipperhey to it.

The earliest drawing of a telescope is a sketch in a letter by Italian scholar Giambattista della Porta (1535–1615) in 1609. Della Porta later claimed he had invented the telescope years before Lipperhey, but he died before he could provide evidence of his claim. In fact, it is likely that long before Lipperhey many lens makers had held two lenses in the right configuration and seen a slightly magnified image, but not realized its potential.

Any uncertainty in the story of the telescope falls away in 1609, when other people heard about the new instrument, made their own, and used it for a novel and world-changing purpose: gazing at the night sky. The first person to note that he had gazed upwards in this way was English astronomer and mathematician Thomas Harriot (1560–1621), who made a sketch of the moon as seen through his telescope on July 26, 1609. Most famously, Galileo Galilei (1564–1542) did the same, and much more, four months later. He published his monumental findings in his book *Sidereus Nuncius* (*The Starry Messenger*) in 1610.

Hans Lipperhey is often also credited with the invention of the microscope, or to be more precise, the compound microscope (consisting of two or more lenses, rather than one). Here again, Zaccharius Janssen probably invented the device around the same time as, if not before, Lippershey. Again, there is no patent for the microscope, because it was inevitable that, at some point, someone would arrange two lenses in the right way to make things look bigger.

Lipperhey's and Janssen's home city of Middelburg was famous for its spectacle makers, thanks to its supply of fine-quality, bubble-free glass and to a superior lens-grinding technique developed in the city. Working with high-quality glass was a novelty in Northern Europe in the seventeenth century the secret of its manufacture had been exported from Italy, which had had the monopoly on fine-quality glass since the thirteenth century.

In a sense, then, along with the lens grinders of Middelburg, the Italian glassmakers of the thirteenth century also deserve credit for these wonderful, world-changing inventions.

LEFT: *Two of Galileo's telescopes, on display at the Museum of the History of Science, Florence. The larger one had a magnification of 20x. The ebony frame below the telescopes houses the actual objective lens through which Galileo gazed into space in 1609 and 1610.*

FAR LEFT: *The Hubble Space Telescope, in orbit above Earth's atmosphere. Hubble has a concave mirror, rather than an objective lens, to gather light. A camera inside takes pictures using that light, producing incredible, clear images of a wide range of astronomical objects.*

CORNELIUS DREBBEL
(1572–OCTOBER 1633)

THE PERSON WHO DESIGNED AND BUILT THE FIRST SUBMARINE, DUTCH INVENTOR CORNELIUS DREBBEL, IS NOT A HOUSEHOLD NAME. BUT HIS BRILLIANT MIND, HIS GRASP OF CHEMICAL PROCESSES AND THE FORCES OF NATURE MADE HIM ONE OF THE MOST PROLIFIC AND BEST-KNOWN INVENTORS OF THE SEVENTEENTH CENTURY.

Cornelius Drebbel was born in Alkmaar, in the Netherlands (then the Dutch Republic), the son of a wealthy farmer. He had little formal schooling, but aged 20 he was apprenticed to the Dutch painter, engraver and publisher Hendrick Goltzius (1558–1617) in Haarlem. During his apprenticeship, Drebbel had the chance to experiment with more than engraving. He learned the art of alchemy, and throughout the rest of his life, his work was dominated by the elements of that art: earth, air, fire and water.

Drebbel moved back to Alkmaar in 1598, and began creating ingenious inventions. In 1604, he demonstrated the one that would bring him fame: a fascinating astronomical clock called the Perpetuum Mobile. In the patent for the device, Drebbel claimed it could run for decades without a visible source of power.

The Perpetuum Mobile displayed the hour, day and date, the phases of the Moon and the position of the Sun and planets. It was powered by changes in air pressure and temperature, a fact that Drebbel was aware of, although at the time he was happy for a bit of mystique to surround his invention. Later in 1604, he was called to England to show it to King James I (1566–1625), and as news spread of this remarkable clock, Drebbel gained notoriety and invitations to show his invention across Europe.

From 1604 until his death, Drebbel created and demonstrated many new and improved inventions. Among them was a process for making an intense scarlet dye, a technology that was to endure well beyond his lifetime. He also invented a thermostatically controlled furnace (the first known autonomous control system); a portable bread oven for the Dutch army; a form of air conditioning, which

TOP LEFT: *Contemporary portrait of Dutch inventor Cornelius Drebbel from an engraving by an unknown artist, published in 1628.*

ABOVE: *Illustration of Drebbel's Perpetuum Mobile clock, from the 1612 book* Dialogue Philosophicall *by English clergyman and author Thomas Tymme (d. 1620). The central sphere (A) represents the Earth, while the upper sphere (B) displays the lunar phases.*

BELOW: *This modern reconstruction of one of Drebbel's submarines sits in Heron Square, Richmond-upon-Thames, London. It was based on design documents found at the Public Records Office in London, and made by a local boatbuilder in 2003.*

The DREBBEL

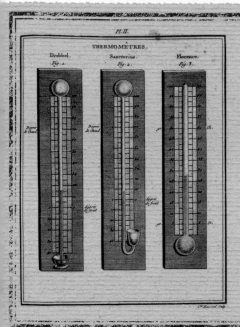

THE DEVELOPMENT OF THERMOMETERS

One of Cornelius Drebbel's most important inventions was a basic thermometer. His instrument relied on the expansion and contraction of air trapped in a glass tube.

Strictly speaking, Drebbel's instrument was a thermoscope — an instrument that gives an indication of temperature while having no scale with which to measure it. At least three other experimenters produced air thermoscopes around the same time, but what set Drebbel's apart was that he used it to control his thermostatic devices. His was the one that had the most influence on scientists in the next generation.

It was Daniel Gabriel Fahrenheit (1686–1736) who invented the prototype of the modern liquid-in-glass thermometer. He also created the first accurate temperature scale, defined by fixed points — one of them was salted ice water, one was his wife's armpit. In the eighteenth and nineteenth centuries, the use of accurate thermometers contributed hugely to scientists' understanding of the behaviour of matter and to the development of the concept of energy.

---

he reportedly demonstrated in the auspicious Westminster Hall in London; and an automatic chicken incubator. He also invented a primitive, though important, thermometer (see box).

Drebbel also experimented with light and lenses: he constructed an early form of projector, and one of the first practical microscopes. Both these devices were made with lenses he had ground using a machine of his own design. Drebbel's microscope was a distinct improvement on the few that already existed, and was important in the development of microscopy.

His most notable achievement, however, was designing, constructing and trialling the invention he is now best known for: the world's first submarine. Sadly, no convincing contemporary illustrations of Drebbel's invention exist, but there are contemporary accounts and modern best guesses of how he might have built it. Between 1620 and 1624, Drebbel built three different versions of his vessel, while working for the English Royal Navy. He tested them in the River Thames in London. Eyewitness accounts suggest that his vessels could stay submerged for hours at a time, diving as deep as 4 to 5 metres (13 to 16 feet) beneath the surface.

The submarines contained large pigskin bladders for buoyancy; these were filled with and emptied of water as necessary. Each craft was a sealed wooden double-hull craft with leather-sealed holes along the sides through which oars protruded. The third and largest vessel could carry 16 people, 12 of them oarsmen. The hull was covered with greased leather to make it watertight. Some accounts suggest that long tubes allowed the oarsmen to breathe. However, there is also evidence that Drebbel may have used a chemical reaction – heating saltpetre (potassium nitrate) – to produce oxygen.

Drebbel tried to convince the English Royal Navy to adopt his submarine for use in warfare. Despite his ongoing relationship with the royal family, however, the Navy was not interested. It would be 150 years before submarines were used for military purposes.

ABOVE: *Drebbel's last submarine is shown only partially submerged in the River Thames, London, in this 1626 illustration by G.H. Tweedale. Legend has it that King James even had a ride in the vessel – in which case he would have been the first monarch ever to travel in a submarine.*

LEFT: *Model of Turtle, the first submarine to be used in warfare. The one-man craft, driven by hand-cranked propellers, was built in 1775 by American inventor David Bushnell (1742–1824), and was used to attach explosives to the hulls of ships.*

BENJAMIN FRANKLIN

(17 JANUARY 1706–17 APRIL 1790)

WHEN THE UNITED STATES OF AMERICA WAS BORN ON 4 JULY 1776, ONE OF THE MEN WHO SIGNED THE DECLARATION OF INDEPENDENCE WAS BENJAMIN FRANKLIN. A FINE STATESMAN, FRANKLIN WAS ALSO AN IMPORTANT FIGURE IN EIGHTEENTH-CENTURY SCIENCE AND INVENTION — JUST THE SORT OF PERSON A NEW NATION NEEDS.

Benjamin Franklin was born in Boston, Massachusetts, USA. He was one of 17 children, and his parents could only afford to send him to school for two years. He was keen to learn, however, and was an avid reader – and at just 12 years old, he became an apprentice at his older brother's printing firm. Following a dispute with his brother five years later, Franklin ran away from home to make a new life in Philadelphia. Penniless to begin with, he managed to find an apprenticeship in a printer's firm there, and soon set up his own printing shop.

By the 1740s, Franklin was very successful – he now owned a publishing company and a newspaper business – and he began to spend increasing amounts of his time on scientific research. Franklin was a strong believer in the idea that science and technology can be used to improve

LEFT: Benjamin Franklin, inventor, scientist and statesman. 1778 portrait by French painter Joseph Duplessis (1725–1802).

society. In 1743, he founded the American Philosophical Society, the nation's first learned society. In the same year, he invented a cleaner, more efficient way of heating the home: the Franklin Stove. Since he intended it to be for the public good, he didn't patent it. In 1749, Franklin retired from business, so that he could spend more time on his research. His work on optics famously led him to invent bifocals, although others probably invented them independently, around the same time. Bifocals are like two pairs of glasses in one, in a split-lens arrangement – ideal for people who need different pairs of glasses for distance and close-up and would otherwise have to keep changing from one pair to another.

Fire prevention was a major concern at the time, since most buildings were still made of wood. In 1736, Franklin had founded one of America's first volunteer fire departments. In 1752, he formed America's first fire insurance company; and came up

ABOVE: Eighteenth-century Franklin-style bifocals, with sliding adjustable arms. In a letter to his friend, English merchant George Whatley, dated 1784, Franklin wrote that he was "happy in the invention of double spectacles", although it is possible someone else had invented them before him.

RIGHT: Coloured lithograph illustrating Franklin's 1752 experiment that proved lightning is an electrical phenomenon. On the ground, beside Franklin, is a Leyden jar to collect electric charge drawn off the thundercloud through the kite string.

with his most famous invention, the lightning rod, aimed at preventing the risk of fire from lightning.

Lightning rods, or lightning conductors, are pointed metal spikes connected to the earth, which draw off electric charge from clouds, dramatically reducing the risk of lightning strikes. When lightning does strike, the rods carry the electricity to the ground, bypassing the building to which they are attached. They may seem like a simple or even insignificant invention today, but at the time, Franklin's invention caused a real buzz and helped to foster the idea that basic insight into natural forces can produce important practical results.

Franklin's fascination with electricity and with lightning led him to carry out his famous kite experiment, in 1752. During a storm, he flew a kite into a thundercloud and drew electric charge down the wet kite string, proving for the first time that lightning is an electrical phenomenon.

Between 1757 and 1775, Franklin spent most of his time travelling between Europe and America, negotiating between the British, the French and the Americans during the turbulent period leading up to American independence. During this time, he became the first person to carry out detailed studies of the Gulf Stream, a warm current of seawater that originates in the Gulf of Mexico and travels across the Atlantic Ocean to Europe. His resulting map of the Gulf Stream helped speed travel and postal services across the ocean.

In addition to his scientific work, Franklin created America's first lending library; he founded America's first hospital (Pennsylvania, 1751) and university (The Library Company, 1731), pushed through some of the earliest environmental regulations and was a vocal advocate of the abolition of slavery. He was also America's first Postmaster General, for which he was commemorated on America's first postage stamp, issued in 1847.

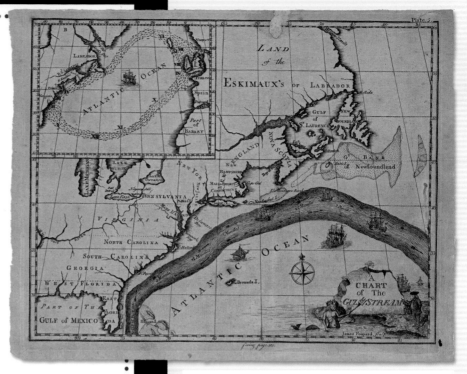

ABOVE: *Franklin's 1786 map of the Gulf Stream. Franklin did not discover the current, but he was the first to study it systematically, after noticing that mail ships took longer crossing the Atlantic from America to Europe than from Europe to America.*

BELOW LEFT: *New York's Empire State Building being struck by lightning. At the very top of the building is a lightning rod that helps to discharge thunderclouds over the city. In addition to draining charge away, the building receives about 100 lightning strikes each year.*

RESEARCHES IN ELECTRICITY

Franklin conceived of the lightning rod after carrying out researches into electricity, a hot topic at the time. In 1747, he set up a laboratory at his own home. In the mid-1740s, scientists in Germany and Holland had invented a way of storing large amounts of electric charge, in a device called a Leyden jar (right). Franklin connected several of these jars together, so that they could produce a much stronger effect.

In five ground-breaking letters to Britain's Royal Society, Franklin laid down the foundations for the proper study of electrical phenomena. He was the first person to use the terms "charge" and "discharge", the first to write about "positive" and "negative" electricity, and the first to understand that electric charge is not "created", but simply transferred from place to place.

JAMES WATT

(19 JANUARY 1736–25 AUGUST 1819)

ONE afternoon in may 1765, scottish engineer James Watt had an idea that changed the world. Watt had hit upon a clever device to make steam engines more efficient and more powerful. It was this device and his other inventions that made steam the driving force of the Industrial Revolution.

English engineer Thomas Newcomen (1663–1729) built the first practical steam engine in 1712 to pump water from coal mines. By the time of Watt's birth, there were nearly a hundred Newcomen engines across Britain, and several more in other countries.

Newcomen's engine relied on atmospheric pressure to push down a piston inside a huge, open-topped vertical cylinder. That could only happen if there was a vacuum inside the cylinder, beneath the piston. Newcomen achieved the necessary vacuum by condensing the steam inside the cylinder back into water, which takes up only a tiny fraction of the volume steam does. A system of valves allowed steam to fill the cylinder, then sprayed in cold water to condense the steam. Having to cool the cylinder down for each stroke of the piston, and then heat it up with steam ready for the next stroke, made the engine incredibly inefficient. It was this fact that Watt addressed that day in 1765.

James Watt was born in Greenock, a town on the River Clyde, west of Glasgow in Scotland. His father was a ship's instrument builder. Using a tool kit his father had given him, Watt became a skilled craftsman from an early age. Following a year working in Glasgow, and a year in London learning the trade of making mathematical instruments such

LEFT: *Portrait of James Watt, painted around 1810. Watt's inventions revolutionized the use of steam power in industry in the 1770s and 1780s.*

BELOW: *Reconstruction of Watt's Workshop at the Science Museum, London, after the contents were removed from Heathfield Hall, Handsworth, in Birmingham. Watt was using the busts on the workbench to test a machine he invented to copy sculptures – a kind of three-dimensional photocopier.*

THE LUNAR SOCIETY

James Watt was a member of a very important society: an informal group of scientists, engineers, industrialists, philosophers, doctors, artists and poets called the Lunar Society.

This group of intellectuals typified the spirit of the Age of Enlightenment – that period of history when people began believing that science, technology and reason could, and should, shape society. Their activities centred on regular meetings, which were often held at the house of Matthew Boulton, also a member. In addition to the meetings, the members of the group were in frequent communication by letter.

The Lunar Society was very important in the transformation of Britain from a rural, agricultural society to an urban, industrial one – it has been described as the revolutionary committee of the Industrial Revolution. The society's name was derived from the fact that the meetings were always held on the Monday closest to full moon: the moonlight made it easier for members to get home afterwards.

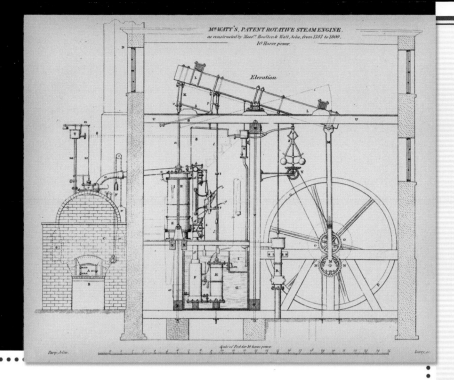

Mr WATT'S, PATENT ROTATIVE STEAM ENGINE.
as constructed by Messrs. Boulton & Watt, Soho, from 1787 to 1800.
10 Horse power.

Elevation

ABOVE: *Technical drawing of a Watt rotative engine from the 1780s. Steam produced in the boiler (left) entered the cylinder, in which the piston moved up and down. On each down stroke, the piston rod pulled down one end of the pivoting beam, the other end of which turned the large flywheel by means of a sun and planet gear.*

BELOW: *Model of an early Savery pumping engine. Steam from the boiler (left) filled the receiver (right), and water rushed into the receiver as the steam condensed. The water was then forced up through another pipe when new steam was admitted to the cylinder.*

ABOVE: *Watt rotative engine at the Science Museum, London. In the background is the cylinder; to the right, the speed-regulating governor (invented by Watt); in the foreground, the flywheel.*

as theodolites and compasses, Watt wanted to set up his own shop. After repairing an instrument for a professor at Glasgow University, he was offered a room there to use as a workshop, and earned a living making and selling musical instruments as well as mathematical ones.

In 1763, Watt began experimenting with a model of a Newcomen engine. He quickly realized just how much fuel, steam and heat Newcomen's design wasted. Watt's great idea of 1765 was the "separate condenser". In Watt's design, the steam was condensed in a chamber connected to but separate from the cylinder. The chamber was held at a lower temperature, so that the cylinder could remain at boiling point. Watt patented his invention in 1769. The engineer and entrepreneur Matthew Boulton (1728–1809) went into business with Watt in 1775. Their partnership lasted until Watt's retirement in 1800 and completely revolutionized the use of steam engines in industry.

Until 1782, steam engines were still used only to pump water in coal mines. That year, on Boulton's request, Watt invented a way to make a steam engine produce a rotary motion, rather than an up-and-down motion – and the resulting "rotative" steam engines were an immediate success. before long, Watt's rotative engines were installed in textile mills, iron foundries, flour mills, breweries and paper mills.

Watt made many other important improvements to steam power – including, in 1782, the "double-acting" engine where steam was admitted to the cylinder alternately above and below the piston, – all choreographed by a clever system of automatic valves. He also invented a steam-pressure gauge and a way of measuring the efficiency of a steam engine. In 1788, he invented the "governor", a device that automatically regulated the speed of an engine.

Watt was also a respected civil engineer, working mostly on canal projects. He is credited with other inventions too, including a popular device for making multiple copies of letters. But steam was his life's work. In honour of his achievements in steam power, the international unit of power, the "watt", is named after him.

Nicéphore Niépce
(7 March 1765–5 July 1833)

LESS THAN 200 YEARS AGO, THERE WAS PRACTICALLY NO WAY OF PRODUCING A LASTING IMAGE OF A SCENE OTHER THAN BY DRAWING OR PAINTING IT. PHOTOGRAPHY, INVENTED BY FRENCH SCIENTIST NICÉPHORE NIÉPCE, HAS HAD A PROFOUND EFFECT ON ART, EDUCATION, HISTORY AND SCIENCE.

Nicéphore Niépce was born in Chalon-sur-Saône, France. His father was a steward to a duke, but little else is known of his childhood. When he was 21, he left home to study at a Catholic oratory school in Angers, where he became interested in physics and chemistry. His first name was originally Joseph; he began using the name Nicéphore, which means "victory-bearer", when he joined the fight against the monarchy in the French Revolution in 1788.

It was in 1793 that Niépce first had the idea of producing permanent images. Around the same time, he and his brother, Claude (1763-1828), conceived of a new type of engine that would use explosions inside a cylinder to drive a piston. Together, they invented the world's first internal combustion engine, the Pyréolophore. Its fuel was a highly flammable

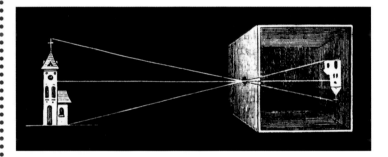

powder of spores from a fungus called lycopodium (which, quite coincidentally, was later used in photographic flash bulbs). They received a patent in 1807, and two years later the brothers entered a government competition to design a replacement for a huge pumping machine on the River Seine in Paris. Their ingenious idea was highly favoured by the judging committee, but in the end the pumping machine was never replaced.

Shortly after its invention in 1796, Niépce learned about a new method of printing illustrations, called lithography, which allowed artists to draw their design directly onto a printing plate, rather than having to etch it into wood or metal. Niépce couldn't draw, so he decided to try and project an image onto the plate instead, hoping to find a way to make the image permanent. To project the image, he turned to an existing technology called the "camera obscura". Popular with Renaissance artists who wanted to produce an accurate representation of a scene, the camera obscura – literally "darkened chamber" – is a simple closed box or room in which a lens casts an image on a screen.

RIGHT: *In 1826, Niépce dissolved bitumen of Judea in lavender oil, spread it on a polished pewter plate, and exposed it in his camera obscura for about eight hours. The result is this,* View from the Window at le Gras, *the oldest photograph in existence.*

LEFT: *Portrait of Niépce painted in 1854 after his death, by French artist Léonard-François Berger (1799–1873). Ironically, there are no photographs of the inventor of photography.*

ABOVE: *An 1825 copy of an earlier print. Niépce soaked the print in varnish to make it translucent, then laid it on a copper plate coated with his bitumen solution. After washing the plate in acid, he was left with an etching, from which to make this print.*

LEFT: *Diagram showing how a pinhole camera obscura works. Making the hole bigger lets more light in, producing a brighter image, but the image becomes blurred. A lens brings it back into focus, and two lenses can bring the image right way up.*

LOUIS DAGUERRE (1787–1851)

After his initial successes with bitumen on pewter plates, Niépce found a way to give better definition to his photographs, or "heliographs" as he called them. He used iodine vapour to make the pewter darken. In 1829, Niépce began collaborating with a French artist, Louis Daguerre. Niépce died in 1833, but by 1837, Daguerre was producing images that only needed a few minutes' exposure. He used copper plates coated with silver iodide, which were "developed" after exposure to mercury vapour and then "fixed" using a strong salt solution.

Daguerre had improved the process so much that he felt justified in calling his photographs daguerreotypes. In 1839, the French Government gave Daguerre's process away, patent-free, as a "gift to the world", and paid Daguerre and Niépce's son a handsome pension. Daguerreotypes became very fashionable, dominating early photography and spurring the development of subsequent photographic technologies.

LEFT: Table Servie *(Set Table) by Niépce. Some experts believe this to be the oldest photograph, dating it to 1822, but it is more likely to be from c.1832. The original was on a glass slide, now broken.*

BELOW: The Ladder, *photographed c.1845 by William Fox Talbot (1800–1877). Talbot invented the calotype process, which involves making prints from negatives.*

Niépce had some success with paper coated with light-sensitive compounds of silver. Images did register on the paper, but they completely blackened when they were exposed to light as they were removed from the camera. Also, this process produced negatives: the parts of the paper where the most light fell became the darkest parts of the resulting image. So Niépce tried using compounds that bleach in sunlight, instead of those that darken. In 1822, Niépce turned to a substance called bitumen of Judea, a thick, tarry substance that hardens and bleaches when exposed to light. His first real successes were in producing permanently etched metal plates. For this, he placed drawings on top of a sheet of glass, which in turn lay on the metal plate coated with bitumen. After exposure to light, for days at a time, he washed away the unhardened bitumen, then treated the plate with nitric acid. The acid etched into the metal wherever the bitumen was not present, leaving a plate from which he could make prints.

Three years later, Niépce began taking pictures of scenes, rather than "photocopying" drawings. He dissolved bitumen in lavender oil and applied the mixture to pewter plates. Then he exposed the plates for several hours in his camera obscura. The bitumen bleached and hardened where light fell, while the unexposed bitumen – representing the darkest parts of the image – was washed away to reveal the dark metal below. These photographs were not negative, but positive, images. The oldest photograph still in existence is *View from the Window at le Gras* (1826), an eerie image of outbuildings taken from the first floor of Niépce's house.

(13 April 1771–22 April 1833)

DURING THE NINETEENTH CENTURY, THE RAILWAYS COMPLETELY REVOLUTIONIZED TRAVEL AND COMMUNICATION FOR MILLIONS OF PEOPLE. THE COMING OF THE RAILWAYS WAS MADE POSSIBLE BY THE INVENTION OF HIGH-PRESSURE STEAM ENGINES BY ENGLISH ENGINEER RICHARD TREVITHICK, WHO ALSO DESIGNED AND BUILT THE FIRST STEAM LOCOMOTIVES.

Richard Trevithick was born in the parish of Illogan, in Cornwall, England. Richard's father was the manager of several local mines, and young Richard spent much of his early life gaining practical knowledge of steam engines. He did not do well at school, but he earned an excellent reputation after he became a mine engineer, aged 19.

At that time, working engines used steam only at atmospheric pressure or slightly above. Trevithick realized early on that steam under high pressure could lead to more compact, more powerful engines. Most people at the time, including steam pioneer James Watt (1736–1819, see page 20), feared "strong steam", believing that the risks of explosion were too high. Trevithick began experimenting with high-pressure steam in the 1790s, and by 1794, he had built his first boiler designed to withstand high pressures, from heavy cast iron.

In 1797, Trevithick built a model steam carriage – and by 1801, he had built a full-size one, nicknamed the "Puffing Devil", which ran successfully in Camborne, Cornwall. The Puffing Devil was destroyed in an accident so, in 1802, Trevithick designed a locomotive that would run on rails. At the time, rails were used with horse-drawn wagons, mainly to transport coal from mines to ports for onward shipping. Trevithick's locomotive, built by the celebrated Coalbrookdale Ironworks, was possibly the first locomotive to run on rails. However, little is known

LEFT: *Trevithick built the first "flue boiler", in which hot exhaust gases pass through tubes inside the water tank and out through the tall chimney. The high-pressure steam produced in these boilers made possible more compact engines.*

BELOW: *Artist's impression of Trevithick's London Steam Carriage of 1803, which was the world's first reliable self-propelled passenger-carrying vehicle. It had a top speed of about 15 kilometres per hour (9 miles per hour) on the flat, and weighed about a tonne when fully laden.*

THE RAINHILL TRIALS

Although Richard Trevithick laid the foundations of the railways, it was not until the 1820s that people began to see steam trains as a serious alternative to horse-drawn transport. The first public railway designed from the start to use steam power was opened between Stockton and Darlington, in northern England, in 1825. Two of the shareholders and engineers on that first railway were father and son George (1781–1848) and Robert Stephenson (1803–1859).

In 1829, the Stephensons entered into the Rainhill Trials, a competition to find a locomotive for the forthcoming Liverpool and Manchester Railway. Their entry was called Rocket, and its many innovations made it the blueprint for all future steam locomotives. Rocket was the only locomotive to complete the ten 5-kilometre (3-mile) round trips required in the competition. When empty of cargo and passengers, it ran at a maximum speed of 47 kilometres per hour (29 miles per hour).

about the locomotive, and only a single letter and drawing relating to it survive.

In 1803, Trevithick built another road vehicle, which he demonstrated in London. It attracted a lot of attention, but it was more expensive, noisier and more inconvenient than horse-drawn carriages, and went no further. In the same year, one of Trevithick's boilers exploded in Greenwich, London. This event could have set back his work; instead Trevithick invented a safety device, a "fusible plug", that he publicized but did not patent, in order to promote high-pressure steam.

The world's first steam train – carriages pulled by a locomotive – was the result of a bet. The owner of the Pen-y-Darren ironworks in Merthyr Tydfil, Wales, bet the manager of a neighbouring ironworks that a steam locomotive could be used to pull carriages filled with iron from his premises to a canal 16 kilometres (9 miles) away. The carriages were normally pulled by horses, so the rails already existed. Trevithick built a locomotive, and in February 1804, it successfully pulled 10.2 tonnes (10 tons) of iron and about 70 people the full distance. Although the rails broke in several places under the weight, the concept of steam trains was proven. A year later, Trevithick built a lighter locomotive for a colliery in Newcastle, but although it worked, it was not put into service.

In 1808, Trevithick built a circular track in Euston, London, to promote the idea of steam trains. This was the world's first fare-paying passenger railway. From July to September that year, Trevithick's locomotive, the *Catch-Me-Who-Can*, ran around its track carrying passengers who paid five shillings for the privilege (later reduced to two shillings). It pulled a single carriage at speeds of about 20 kilometres per hour (12 miles per hour).

Trevithick also built a steam-powered dredging machine; powered a barge using one of his engines; and in 1812, he built an engine to thresh corn. In addition he invented an early propeller for steamboats and a device for heating homes, and he worked as an engineer on a tunnel under the River Thames in London, as well as on various projects in the silver mines of South America. But it is his pioneering contributions to the birth of the railways for which Richard Trevithick will be remembered.

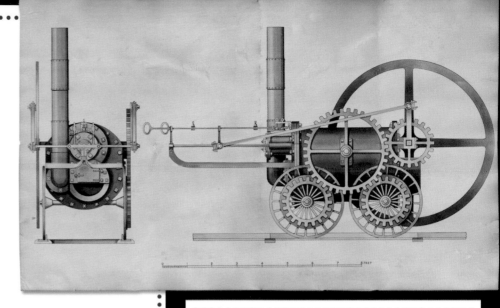

ABOVE: *Trevithick's Coalbrookdale Locomotive – the world's first locomotive to run on rails. The Coalbrookdale was built for a colliery in Newcastle, in 1803. This contemporary illustration is the only source of information about it.*

LEFT: *The Pen-y-Darren Locomotive, built in 1804, pulling wagons. The locomotive was formed by lifting one of Trevithick's existing stationary engines onto wheels at the Pen-y-Darren ironworks in Wales. It ran only three times, because it was too heavy for the iron rails. After the engine's trials, the railway returned to using horse power..*

RIGHT: *Trevithick's demonstration of the potential of steam trains in Euston, London, in 1808 – later called "The Steam Circus". The locomotive was called* Catch-Me-Who-Can, *because – to show that travel by steam would be faster – Trevithick raced it in a 24-hour race against horses, and won.*

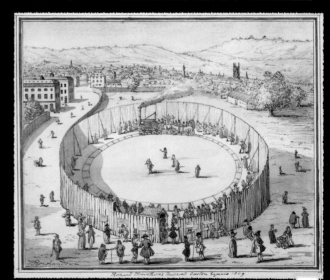

MICHAEL FARADAY
(22 SEPTEMBER 1791–25 AUGUST 1867)

ELECTRIC MOTORS, GENERATORS AND TRANSFORMERS HAVE HELPED TO DEFINE THE MODERN WORLD. ENGLISH CHEMIST AND PHYSICIST MICHAEL FARADAY MADE THE FIRST EXAMPLES OF EACH OF THESE DEVICES. MORE PURE SCIENTIST THAN INVENTOR, FARADAY NEVERTHELESS HAD A PRACTICAL BENT, WHICH LED HIM TO FIND INNOVATIVE WAYS OF USING SOME OF THE INCREDIBLE THINGS HE CREATED IN HIS LABORATORY.

Michael Faraday was born in Newington Butts, in London. Unlike most scientists of his day, he was not born into a wealthy family and did not benefit from much formal education. At the age of 13, his family secured an apprenticeship for him as a bookbinder.

Faraday took the opportunity to read many of the books he bound, and from these he developed an interest in science. In 1812, he was given tickets to a lecture by English chemist Humphrey Davy (1778–1829), who was about to retire from the Royal Institution in London. Keen to move out of bookbinding, Faraday wrote up his notes from the lecture, bound them and presented them to Davy in the hope of being offered a job. When a position became available, Davy employed Faraday as his assistant.

After Davy's retirement, Faraday travelled across Europe with him, meeting some of the most important scientists of the day. On his return, Faraday experimented in the field of chemistry, making several discoveries and inventing the earliest version of the Bunsen burner. A chance discovery in 1819/20 by Danish experimenter Hans Christian Ørsted (1777–1851) was to take Faraday in a new direction. Ørsted had discovered that whenever electric current flows, it produces magnetic forces. In 1821, Davy and his colleague William Wollaston (1766–1828) tried to use this phenomenon to make an electric motor, but they could not get it to work.

Later in 1821, Faraday succeeded where Davy and Wollaston had failed. He suspended a wire over a magnet in a cup of mercury. The wire rotated around the magnet whenever electric current flowed through it, because of the interaction between the magnetic field produced by the wire and the magnetic field of the magnet. Crude though it was, this was the precursor of all electric motors, which today are found in washing machines, drills and a host of other machines and appliances. When Faraday published his results, he failed to credit Davy, and the

LEFT: *Replica of apparatus used by Faraday in 1831 that changes movement energy into electrical energy. The permanent bar magnet moved in and out of the coil of wire "induces" a voltage in the solenoid. If the coil is part of a closed circuit, a current flows.*

BELOW: *Replica of Faraday's induction ring – the world's first transformer, consisting of two long wires coiled around an iron ring. A changing electric current flowing in one coil produces a changing magnetic field in the iron ring, which induces a voltage in the other coil.*

LEFT: *Faraday's Giant Electromagnet (1830), under the table in a mock-up of his laboratory at the Royal Institution, London. It was with this magnet that Faraday discovered that materials such as water and wood are repelled weakly by a strong magnet – a property called "diamagnetism".*

resulting fuss caused Faraday to stop working on electromagnetism until after Davy's death in 1829.

In 1831 in the basement of the Royal Institution, Faraday made a series of groundbreaking discoveries with batteries and wires. First, he discovered that a magnetic field produced by electric current in one wire can create, or "induce", electric current in another wire nearby. Faraday wound two long insulated wires around a circular iron ring, which intensified the effect; what he had made was the world's first transformer. Today, transformers are a vital part of the electricity distribution network, and they are also found in many home appliances, including mobile-phone chargers and televisions.

A month later, Faraday fixed a copper disc between the poles of a strong magnet and attached wires to the disc, one via the axle and one via a sliding contact. When he rotated the disc, an electric current was produced in the wires. This was the world's first electric generator. A year later, French instrument maker Hippolyte Pixii (1808–1835) read about Faraday's discovery and made an improved generator using coils of wire spinning close to a magnet's poles. Today, generators that supply huge amounts of electric power from power stations and wind turbines can trace their lineage directly back to Pixii's design.

In addition to his research and his inventions, Faraday instigated regular Friday discourses and the celebrated Christmas lectures at the Royal Institution; he himself was an inspiring lecturer. Later in his career, Faraday campaigned to clean up air and river pollution, and he was called upon to improve lighthouse technology and to investigate mining disasters. The most important contributions Faraday made, however, were those he made in the basement of the Royal Institution.

ABOVE: *Michael Faraday lecturing at the Royal Institution. In 1825, Faraday instigated two series of public lectures that are still a feature of the institution: a series of Friday evening discourses and the annual Christmas Lectures, aimed at young people.*

JAMES CLERK MAXWELL (1831–1879)

During his researches with magnetism and electromagnetism, Michael Faraday became the first to describe "fields" of force. Several of his contemporaries expressed his discoveries in the precise language of mathematics, which Faraday's lack of formal education prevented him from doing. Most notable among these mathematical physicists was Scottish mathematician James Clerk Maxwell.

In the 1850s, Maxwell derived four equations that comprehensively describe the behaviour and interaction of electricity and magnetism. In 1864, Maxwell combined the equations, and the result was a single equation that describes wave motion. The speed of the wave described by the equation worked out to be exactly what experimenters had found the speed of light to be. Maxwell had shown that light is an electromagnetic wave. He went on to predict that light is a small part of a whole spectrum of electromagnetic radiation, a prediction that was confirmed in 1887 by the discovery of radio waves by German physicist Heinrich Hertz (1857–1894).

CHARLES BABBAGE
(26 December 1791–18 October 1871)

LONG BEFORE THE INVENTION OF THE MODERN COMPUTER, A DETERMINED GENIUS NAMED CHARLES BABBAGE DESIGNED MACHINES THAT WOULD CARRY OUT COMPLICATED MATHEMATICAL OPERATIONS, AND INVENTED THE WORLD'S FIRST PROGRAMMABLE COMPUTING DEVICE. BABBAGE WAS A BRILLIANT MATHEMATICIAN, BUT HE ALSO CONTRIBUTED TO THE DEVELOPMENT OF BUSINESS EFFICIENCY AND RAILWAY TRAVEL.

As a child, Babbage was extremely inquisitive. In his autobiography, he wrote that whenever he had a new toy, he would ask his mother "What's inside it?", and would always break things open to find out how they worked. This curiosity gave him an early understanding of machines and mechanisms.

In 1810, he went to study mathematics at Trinity College, Cambridge University. At the time, mathematicians and engineers relied on books filled with tables of numbers to carry out calculations. There were tables of trigonometric functions (sine, cosine and tangent) and tables of logarithms. The books contained hundreds of tables, and each table contained thousands of numbers. The values in the tables were worked out by hand, by "computers" – a word that meant "people who compute". In 1812, Babbage moved college, to Peterhouse. In the library there, he realized that there were large numbers of mistakes in the numerical tables, and that they were down to human error. At the time, various mechanical calculating machines existed, but they were limited in what they could do. So Babbage envisaged a machine that would be able to calculate these tables at speed and remove the risk of human error.

In 1822, Babbage presented to the Royal Astronomical Society a proposal to build a calculating machine. The society granted Babbage money to set about making his machine, and he hired an engineer to oversee the job. In a workshop close to Babbage's house, with machine tools painstakingly designed by Babbage himself, the engineer set to work. It was an enormous task, and Babbage repeatedly asked for, and was granted, more money from the British Government.

Babbage called his proposed device the Difference Engine. It was never finished, because of a dispute between Babbage and the engineer – and perhaps also because it was so complicated. The Government officially abandoned the project in 1842. Babbage later improved

RIGHT: *Babbage's collection of mathematical tables. His engines were designed to make these redundant.*

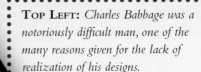

B. H. Babbage del.

TOP LEFT: *Charles Babbage was a notoriously difficult man, one of the many reasons given for the lack of realization of his designs.*

ABOVE: *Babbage's Difference Engine No.1. It was built in 1832 by Joseph Clement, a skilled toolmaker and draughtsman. It was a decimal digital machine; the value of a number represented by the positions of toothed wheels marked with decimal numbers.*

ANALYTICAL ENGINE

Babbage's Analytical Engine was the first known design for a mechanical, general all-purpose computer. Although never built, the concepts it utilized in its design were at least 100 years before their time. Programs and data would be input using punched cards. Output consisted of a printer, a curved plotter and a bell. The machine's memory would be capable of holding 1,000 numbers of 50 decimal digits each. The programming language it was to use was very similar to that used in the early computers 100 years later. It used loops and conditional branching and was thus Turing-complete long before Alan Turing's concept (see page 56). Although Babbage's direct influence on the later development of computing is argued greatly, Howard H. Aiken — the primary engineer behind IBM's 1944 Harvard Mark I (the first large-scale automatic digital computer in the United States) — said of Babbage's writings on the Analytical Engine, "There's my education on computers, right there; this is the whole thing, everything took out of a book."

BELOW: A design sketched by Babbage for part of his Analytical Engine.

his design, which he called Difference Engine 2. In 1991, London's Science Museum followed Babbage's design and constructed it; in 2005, they added a printer that had also been part of Babbage's original design. Both machines worked perfectly.

In 1827, his father, his wife and one of his sons died, and Babbage stopped work and took time to travel in Europe. While he was travelling, he dreamed up a more general calculating machine, which would be able to follow sets of instructions. Babbage envisaged a machine that would have input via punched cards, would be able to store answers, and would have a printer that would output the results. By 1835, he had produced the first of many designs for an "Analytical Engine" – the forerunner to the modern programmable computer. His design was expressed in 500 large engineering drawings, a thousand pages of engineering calculations and thousands of pages of sketches. Unfortunately, this machine was also never finished.

Babbage's designs inspired the pioneers of the modern computer, and this is what he is remembered for, but he also had a significant influence on other fields. While he was travelling in Europe in the 1820s, Babbage toured factories and studied the manufacturing process. In 1832, he published a book called *On the Economy of Machinery and Manufacture*, which was the beginning of studies into the efficiency of business and industry – what is now called operational research. He applied his methods to mail in Britain, and the result was the world's first cheap and efficient national postal system.

He also studied the efficiency of the railways, which were in their infancy at the time. He invented a special carriage filled with equipment that would record the bumps in the tracks during a journey, and a device to move objects off the track ahead of a train – affectionately called a cowcatcher.

RIGHT: Babbage's cowcatcher in use on a steam locomotive in Pakistan's North-West Frontier Province. The concept was used on trains around the world.

JOSEPH LISTER
(5 APRIL 1827–10 FEBRUARY 1912)

UNTIL THE LATE NINETEENTH CENTURY, PATIENTS UNDERGOING EVEN MINOR SURGERY HAD ABOUT AS MUCH CHANCE OF DYING AFTERWARDS AS THEY DID OF SURVIVING. ENGLISH SURGEON JOSEPH LISTER DRAMATICALLY IMPROVED PATIENTS' CHANCES IN THE 1870S, BY INTRODUCING ANTISEPTICS INTO SURGERY.

Joseph Lister was born in Upton, in Essex, England, to a wealthy Quaker family. His father was a man of science, who made significant improvements to microscope design. Joseph studied the arts and then medicine at University College, London. Although born and educated in England, he spent most of his career in Scotland.

In 1856, Lister became an assistant surgeon at the Edinburgh Royal Infirmary. Four years later, he was appointed Professor of Surgery at Glasgow University Medical School. In 1861, Lister was put in charge of a new building with surgical wards at Glasgow Royal Infirmary. At the time, around half of the patients died as a result of surgery – open wounds often festered, becoming badly infected and inflamed and full of pus. Untreated, this "wound sepsis" was often life-threatening. The prevailing explanation of infection was the so-called "miasma theory": the idea that polluted air was the cause of disease. In the filthy air of the disease-ridden cities of the nineteenth century, this was an easy connection to make. But it badly missed the point: believing that polluted air caused disease, surgeons carried out operations without washing their hands and surgical wards were not clean.

In 1865, Lister read a report by French chemist and microbiologist Louis Pasteur (1822–1895) suggesting that fermentation and rotting are caused by airborne micro-organisms. Pasteur also showed how micro-organisms can be killed by heat, filtration or chemical attack. When Lister heard of Pasteur's work, he realized that airborne micro-organisms might be causing wounds to turn septic. He had heard that carbolic acid (phenol, C_6H_5OH) had been used to stop sewage from smelling bad, and had also been sprayed onto fields, where it reduced the incidence of disease in cows. And so, he and his surgeons began applying carbolic acid solution to wounds, and using dressings that had been soaked in a the same solution. In 1869, he developed a spray that would fill the air with carbolic acid – the aim being to kill airborne germs. Lister also told his surgeons to wash their hands before and after operations and to wash their surgical instruments in carbolic acid solution. His results were impressive: his surgical wards remained free of sepsis for nine months, and Lister had proved that carbolic acid was an effective antiseptic.

ABOVE: *Glasgow slum, 1868. As in all large cities at the time, poor sanitation and overcrowding led to the spread of infectious diseases. This gave rise to the miasma theory, in which "foul air" was blamed for disease. The miasma theory was eventually superseded by the germ theory of disease.*

LEFT: *Carbolic acid solution spray, used to sterilize tools and open wounds, as pioneered by Joseph Lister. This example is from France; French surgeons were quick to adopt Lister's sterile surgical procedures, in part because it had saved many lives in the Franco-Prussian war.*

ABOVE: *French chemist and microbiologist Louis Pasteur in his laboratory, in a classic 1885 painting by Finnish-Swedish painter Albert Eledfelt (1854–1905). During the 1870s, Pasteur carried out a series of brilliant experiments that higlighted the existence – and effects – of airborne microbes.*

ABOVE RIGHT: *Portrait of Ignaz Semmelweis on a 1965 Austrian stamp commemorating the hundredth anniversary of his death.*

Other surgeons were slow to copy Lister's procedures, largely because many were reluctant to accept the idea that disease can be caused by micro-organisms – an idea known as the "germ theory of disease". When, gradually, surgeons did begin using his techniques, post-operative survival rates increased dramatically. It was after surgeons in the Franco-Prussian War of 1870–1871 used Lister's techniques, saving the lives of many wounded soldiers, that Lister's fame spread across Europe, and he began to receive the recognition he deserved. In 1877, Lister moved back to King's College, London, where he managed to convince many of the still-sceptical surgeons by successfully performing a complex knee replacement operation that had nearly always proved fatal. He continued to experiment tirelessly on improving surgical techniques and reducing mortality until his retirement in 1893.

Although Lister is famous for his antiseptic methods, he also worked on "aseptic" ones: attempting to keep operating theatres free of germs rather than killing them. Scottish surgeon Lawson Tait (1845–1899) defined modern aseptic surgical practices – even though he was not convinced of the existence of germs. Nevertheless, Lister's pioneering investigations into wound sepsis, his application of the germ theory of disease and his success in reducing mortality make his contributions to surgery of utmost importance.

IGNAZ SEMMELWEIS (1818–1865)

Nearly 30 years before Joseph Lister's pioneering work on antiseptic surgery, a Hungarian obstetrician, Ignaz Semmelweis, demonstrated the importance of washing hands. He worked in maternity wards at the Vienna General Hospitsal, in Austria. In wards attended by doctors and medical students, a disease called puerperal fever typically claimed the lives of about 20 per cent of women after childbirth, while in midwife-only wards, the incidence of puerperal fever was much lower. Semmelweis realized that the doctors and students – who did not wash their hands between operations or even after dissecting corpses – were unwittingly transferring infections from one patient to another. In 1847, Semmelweis began a regime of washing hands with a solution of chlorinated water, and managed to reduce the mortality to below one per cent. Unfortunately, the medical community dismissed Semmelweis's results, and his work was quickly forgotten.

BELOW: *Joseph Lister, centre, directing the use of his carbolic spray during a surgical operation, around 1865. Note the use of a cloth soaked in ether as an anaesthetic (left).*

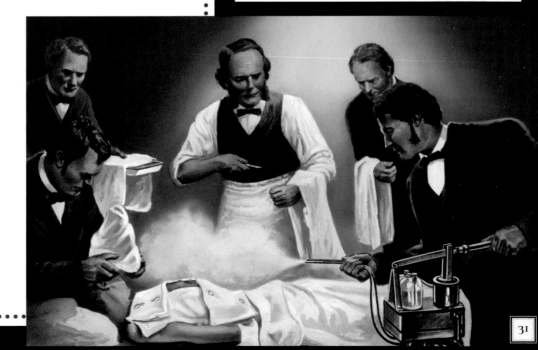

KARL BENZ

(25 NOVEMBER 1844–4 APRIL 1929)

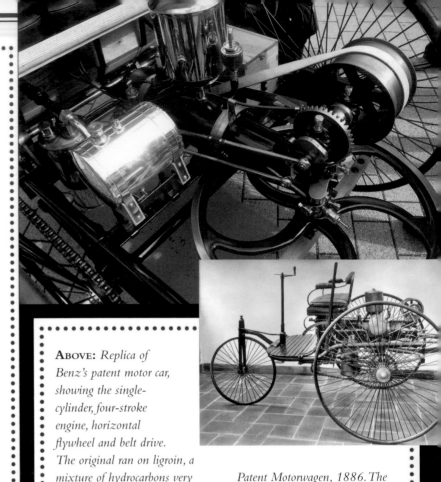

THE PERSON RESPONSIBLE FOR DESIGNING THE FIRST TRUE MOTOR CAR, GERMAN ENGINEER KARL BENZ, HAD NO IDEA WHAT EFFECT HIS INVENTION WOULD HAVE ON THE WORLD. BY INCREASING MOBILITY, LESS THAN 100 YEARS AFTER THE RISE OF THE RAILWAYS, THE MOTOR CAR ONCE AGAIN REVOLUTIONIZED PATTERNS OF WORK AND PLAY AND THE DISTRIBUTION OF GOODS, AND ITS RAPID UPTAKE IN THE TWENTIETH CENTURY CHANGED THE LANDSCAPE QUICKLY AND DRAMATICALLY.

Karl Benz was born in Karlsruhe, Baden (now in Germany). His father died when Karl was just two years old, but his mother encouraged him greatly, working hard to put him through grammar school and the Karlsruhe Polytechnische Schule (Institute of Technology). It was his dream from early on to invent a form of transport that would run without horses and off rails.

The idea of self-propelled road vehicles was already popular before Benz was born. Some engineers had made "cars" – mostly steam carriages and electric vehicles; all of them were adaptations of horse-drawn carts and none was particularly effective. The most crucial invention in the development of the motor car was the internal combustion engine. In a steam engine, the combustion – the

ABOVE: *Photograph of Karl Benz, taken in the 1880s. Born "Karl", Benz began spelling his name "Carl" in the 1890s. His patent DRP 37435, for a "gas-powered vehicle", is dated 29 January 1886, and is often referred to as the "birth certificate of the motor car".*

ABOVE: *Replica of Benz's patent motor car, showing the single-cylinder, four-stroke engine, horizontal flywheel and belt drive. The original ran on ligroin, a mixture of hydrocarbons very similar to petrol. Also visible are the fuel tank, in the foreground, and the cooling water tank.*

ABOVE RIGHT: *Photograph of the original, and unique, Benz Patent Motorwagen, 1886. The car was converted to a four-wheel vehicle in the 1890s, then in 1903, it was returned to its original form. It is now on display at the Deutsches Museum, in Munich, Germany.*

HENRY FORD (1863–1947)

For 20 years after Karl Benz's Patent Motorwagen, motor cars were not available to most people. The fact that each one had to be made individually kept the cost high, which in turn kept demand low. In 1908, American entrepreneur Henry Ford set out to change that, when he introduced what he called "a car for the great multitude".

The affordable Ford Model T was a real breakthrough, being made from interchangeable parts in a factory with tools laid out in an efficient arrangement. From 1913, the cars were manufactured on assembly lines. One of Ford's employees had seen how effective production lines could be when he visited a meat-packing factory in Chicago. The application of the idea to the motor-car industry brought costs down dramatically, made Henry Ford incredibly rich and had a rapid and profound effect on the world of the twentieth century.

fire that heats the steam – is produced outside the cylinder. The first practical engines in which combustion took place inside the cylinder, and drove a piston directly, appeared in the 1850s. The most important was invented in 1859 by Belgian engineer Étienne Lenoir (1822–1900).

The next step towards motor cars proper was the "four-stroke" engine designed by German inventor Nikolaus Otto (1832–1891) in 1876. The four strokes – intake of the fuel-air mixture; compression of that mixture; ignition; and exhaust – still form the basis of petrol engines today. Otto's engine was the first real alternative to the steam engine.

Karl Benz closely followed developments in engine design after leaving college, and worked towards his dream of building a motor car. He had been employed on various mechanical engineering projects, and in 1871 had moved to the nearby city of Mannheim. In the 1870s, Benz designed a reliable two-stroke petrol engine (in which the four operations of the four-stroke engine are combined into one upward and one downward stroke), for which he was granted a patent in 1879. Four years later, he formed a company with two other people: Benz & Company Rheinische Gasmotoren-Fabrik. The company began as a bicycle repair shop, and quickly grew when it began making machines and engines.

Benz & Company did well, giving Benz the time and the confidence he needed to pursue his dream. By the end of 1885,

Benz's car was ready. It was a three-wheeled carriage powered by a single-cylinder four-stroke engine, which he had created specially. Benz's motor car incorporated several important innovations of his own design. These included an electric starter coil, differential gears, a basic clutch and a water-cooling system for the engine. Despite his hard work and his obvious brilliance, Benz had not quite worked out how to achieve steering with four wheels. He took the easy option and had three wheels, the single front wheel being turned by a "tiller"-type handle.

Benz applied for a patent in January 1886, and it was granted in November of that year. His application was successful because his motor car had been designed from the start as a self-powered vehicle, and not simply as a cart with an engine attached.

After a few improvements, including the world's first carburettor, the first Benz Patent Motorwagen was sold in 1887. Benz began production of the car, and advertised it for sale in 1888; it was the first commercially available production car in history. Uptake was very slow, however, so Benz's wife Bertha (1849–1944) decided to try to raise awareness. In August 1888, she drove with her two sons from Mannheim to her home town of Pforzheim and back – a total distance of nearly 200 kilometres (120 miles). The stunt generated a great deal of publicity – and thanks at least in part to that publicity, Benz's Motorwagen became a real success. The age of motoring had begun.

RIGHT: *By 1888, Benz had improved his design, and began producing cars in greater numbers. French engineer and entrepreneur Émile Roger, in Paris, held the sole rights to sell Benz's cars outside Germany, and helped to popularize the vehicle.*

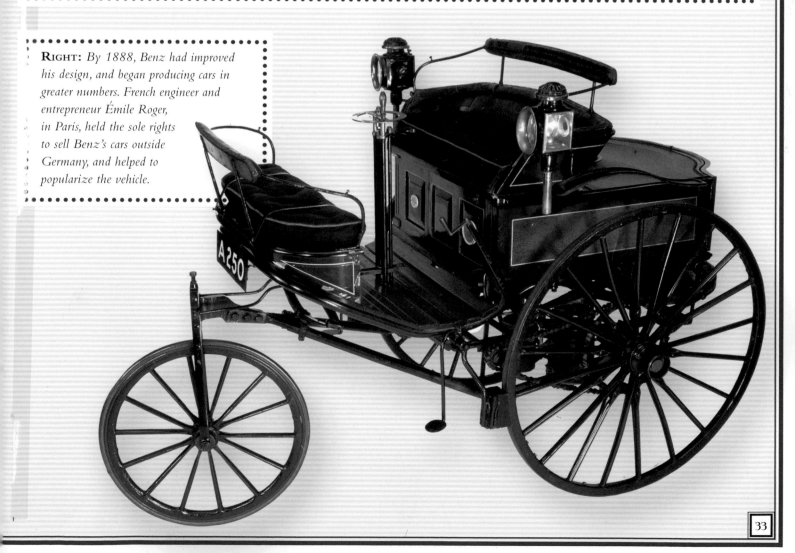

THOMAS EDISON

(11 February 1847–18 October 1931)

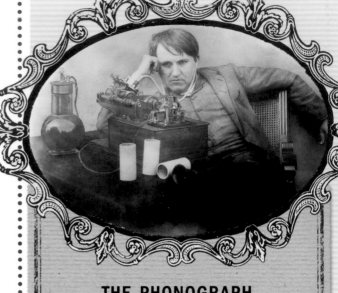

For the sheer number of important inventions he pioneered, Thomas Edison is one of the best-known and most prolific inventors of all time. He was granted a total of 1,093 US patents, but perhaps his greatest invention of all was something he could not patent: organized, systematic research.

Home-schooled from the age of 12, Edison set up his first laboratory in his bedroom at his family's home in Port Huron, Michigan. Much of his early effort was dedicated to improving the telegraph, a system that had revolutionized long-distance communication in the 1840s. When he was 14, Edison built a working telegraph at home; by the age of 16, he was working as a telegraph operator at his local telegraph office; and for the next five years he travelled, working at a number of different telegraph offices in several different cities. Eventually, he decided to devote all his time to inventing.

Edison's first successful invention was the "Universal Stock Ticker" (1870) – a device with which dealers could receive the current share prices across the telegraph system, from the New York Stock Exchange. He sold the rights to this invention, and with the money he made, he set up a workshop in Newark, New Jersey, in which he employed 80 people. One of his employees was 16-year-old Mary Stilwell, who became his first wife in 1871.

In 1873, he invented the "Quadruplex Telegraph", which made it possible to transmit and receive four telegraph signals simultaneously on a single wire. He sold the rights to this invention to Western Union – it saved them millions of dollars in wiring – and the proceeds helped him move his workshop to new premises. In 1876, Edison bought 34 acres (14 hectares) of land in the countryside of Menlo Park, New Jersey, where he set up a full research and development laboratory – the first of its kind anywhere in the

THE PHONOGRAPH

In July 1877 Edison came up with an idea for a device that would make it possible to record and play back sounds. One of his researchers set about trying to make it, and in November Edison recited the first verse of the poem "Mary Had a Little Lamb". To everyone's amazement, the device played back Edison's voice clearly. The phonograph indented sound vibrations on to a sheet of tinfoil wrapped around a cylinder, turned by a hand crank.

Top Right: *Thomas Edison in 1889, seen here listening to recordings made on his phonograph.*

Right: *The galvanizing room in Edison's Menlo Park laboratory. His early electric bulbs can be seen on the table.*

world. At Menlo Park, Edison set about trying to improve the recently-invented telephone. In 1877, he invented a sensitive microphone, filled with compressed carbon, which improved the distance over which telephone calls could be made. His invention was part of nearly every telephone until the 1970s.

As an offshoot of his research into the telephone, Edison and his team invented a device for recording sound: the phonograph. It was an instant success, and Edison travelled extensively to demonstrate his new invention. He was even called to the White House to show it to the then US President, Rutherford Hayes. One journalist referred to Edison as the Wizard of Menlo Park – a name that stuck.

Perhaps the most important invention to come out of Menlo Park was the light bulb. As is true of nearly all his inventions, Edison did not actually invent the light bulb: he made significant improvements that made it practicable for the first time. His use of a carbonized bamboo filament meant a bulb would light for 40 hours instead of just a few minutes. He demonstrated the new technology in December 1879, lighting the workshop in a public demonstration.

Edison set up a bulb-making factory at Menlo Park, and his success with electric light led him to work on a system to distribute electric power. He patented the system in 1880, and by 1882, he had set up a power station at Pearl Street, New York.

In 1884, Edison's wife died. He married again, to Mina Miller, in 1886. The following year, Edison moved his operation to a new laboratory in West Orange, also in New Jersey. He headed the West Orange laboratory until his death in 1931. During this period, his research team invented the first device for showing moving pictures (using 35mm sprocketed film, which later became the film industry standard), a new type of battery, a device for separating iron ore, an all-concrete house, and an electric locomotive.

After Edison died, US President Herbert Hoover encouraged Americans to turn off their lights for one minute, in tribute to the contributions made by America's greatest inventor.

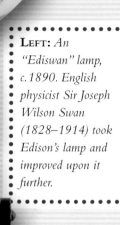

LEFT: *An "Ediswan" lamp, c. 1890. English physicist Sir Joseph Wilson Swan (1828–1914) took Edison's lamp and improved upon it further.*

BELOW: *The Dynamo Room at Pearl Street Station, New York. Pearl Street, the first central power plant in the US, was built by Edison's Electric Illuminating Company and started generating electricity on 4 September 1882. By 1884 it was serving 508 customers and powering 10,164 lamps.*

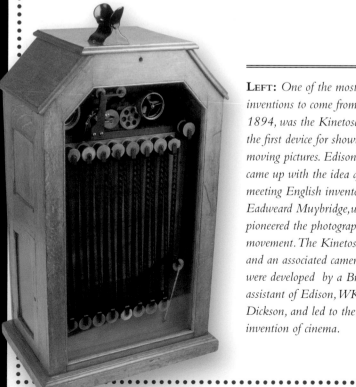

LEFT: *One of the most important early inventions to come from West Orange, in 1894, was the Kinetoscope, the first device for showing moving pictures. Edison came up with the idea after meeting English inventor Eadweard Muybridge, who pioneered the photography of movement. The Kinetoscope and an associated camera were developed by a British assistant of Edison, WKL Dickson, and led to the invention of cinema.*

ALEXANDER GRAHAM BELL

(3 MARCH 1847–2 AUGUST 1922)

PROBABLY THE MOST LUCRATIVE PATENT OF ALL TIME WAS AWARDED TO A SCOTTISH-CANADIAN-AMERICAN AND INVENTOR IN 1876, FOR A DEVICE THAT HAD THE MAGICAL ABILITY TO TRANSMIT THE SOUND OF THE HUMAN VOICE ACROSS LONG DISTANCES. THE INVENTOR'S NAME WAS ALEXANDER GRAHAM BELL, AND THE DEVICE WAS THE TELEPHONE.

Alexander Graham Bell was born in Edinburgh, Scotland. His father and grandfather were pioneers in the field of speech and elocution, and his mother had a condition that resulted in progressive hearing loss. These influences inspired Bell to study language and the human voice. The young Bell attended a prestigious school in Edinburgh, and when he left aged 16, he taught music and elocution before studying in Edinburgh and London. After his studies, Bell taught deaf people to speak, using a method his father had developed, and it was during this time he began experiments in the transmission of sound using electricity.

Bell lost both his brothers to tuberculosis, and in 1870 his own precarious state of health deteriorated. His parents decided the family should emigrate to Canada. Within a year of arriving, Bell had become a Canadian citizen, and his health had improved. The family settled on a farm, and Bell continued his experiments with sound and electricity. He spent time teaching deaf people in Montreal, Canada, and in various American cities. Eventually, he settled in Boston, where he founded a school for the deaf and became professor of vocal physiology at Boston University. However, in 1873, becoming increasingly preoccupied with his attempts to transmit sound with electricity, he resigned his position. He retained two deaf people as private students; as luck would have it, their wealthy parents became interested in what he was trying to achieve, and helped fund his work.

By 1874, Bell had built a device called a harmonic telegraph, which was designed to transmit several telegraph messages at the same time through a single wire. Each message was sent as pulses of electricity with a distinct frequency of alternating current. Bell's financial backers were keen for him to perfect his device, but Bell was much more interested in trying to adapt his device to transmit the human voice through a wire, something that many thought was impossible. In 1875,

LEFT: *Replica of Bell's 1875 experimental telephone transmitter. Speech sounds caused the stretched parchment drum to vibrate, and the metal spring with it. A magnet attached to the spring produced an alternating electric current in the coil above it – one that matched the vibrations of the sound waves.*

LEFT: *Alexander Graham Bell, seated, in New York, on 18 October 1892, at the opening of the first long-distance telephone service. The line connected New York and Chicago, in the USA: a distance of about 1,140 kilometres (710 miles).*

RIGHT: *In 1877, news of Bell's success in transmitting speech spread worldwide. Britain's Queen Victoria asked Bell to demonstrate it at her residence on the Isle of Wight. This telephone and "terminal panel" were part of the resulting installation.*

Bell was getting close, but his knowledge of electricity was lacking. Fortunately, that year he met an electrical technician called Thomas Watson (1854–1934), whom he engaged as his assistant.

When Bell was granted the patent for the telephone, his device had not yet transmitted any speech. But three days later, on 10 March 1876, Bell and Watson achieved success. Bell, in one room, spoke into the device, and in an adjoining room, Watson heard the now famous words, "Mr Watson, come here – I want to see you." In the following months, Bell and Watson made improvements to the microphone, and his device transmitted speech over increasing distances – and began to generate huge interest from scientists and the press. In 1877, he and his financial backers formed the Bell Telephone Company.

Bell's inventions were not restricted to the telegraph and the telephone. He improved Edison's most famous creation: an early sound-recording device called the phonograph. He also invented record-breaking speedboats that rose up out of the water on submerged "wings" called hydrofoils, a chamber to help people with respiratory problems breathe (an early version of the iron lung) and the first metal detector. In his later years, he spent a great deal of time and effort experimenting with flight. The invention of which he was most proud, however, was the photophone, a device that transmitted sound using light rather than electricity. In 1880, Bell's photophone made the first ever wireless transmission of speech, across a distance of more than 210 metres (230 yards). Although his idea never took off at the time, it is similar to the way telephone signals are transmitted today using laser light passing through optical fibres.

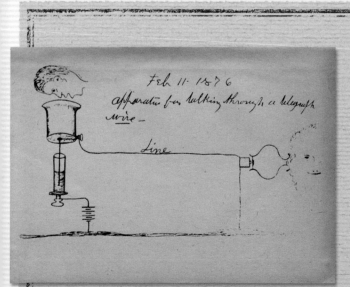

ELISHA GRAY (1831–1901)

Alexander Graham Bell's company fought a total of 587 lawsuits over priority in the invention of the telephone during the 1880s and '90s. The company won them all, ultimately due to the fact that no one had claimed priority until many months after Bell was awarded his patent. However, some controversy remains over Bell and one of his competitors at the time: prolific American inventor Elisha Gray.

On the same day as Bell filed his patent, 14 February 1876, Gray filed a patent "caveat" at the same office, for a very similar device. There is evidence that Bell had sight of Gray's application. In Bell's first successful experiment, he used a water-based microphone Gray had designed. But he never used it in public demonstrations, probably because he knew he should not have known about it. Instead he used his own, less effective, electromagnetic receiver.

GEORGE EASTMAN

((12 July 1854–14 March 1932)

IN ITS FIRST FIFTY YEARS, PHOTOGRAPHY WAS THE PRESERVE OF A RELATIVELY SMALL NUMBER OF PROFESSIONALS AND ENTHUSIASTIC AMATEURS. IT WAS EXPENSIVE, TIME-CONSUMING, AWKWARD AND VERY SPECIALIZED. ALL THAT CHANGED IN 1888, WHEN AMERICAN INVENTOR GEORGE EASTMAN BEGAN SELLING A CHEAPER CAMERA, WHICH WAS ALSO EASIER TO USE.

George Eastman was born on a small farm in New York State, USA. When he was five years old, the family moved to the city of Rochester, also in New York. His father died when George was just eight years old, and the family fell on hard times. As a result, George had to leave school aged 13, to find a job. He was keen to learn, though, and was largely self-taught.

Eastman's interest in photography was sparked at age 24 when, while working as a bank clerk, he planned a trip abroad. A colleague suggested he take a record of his trip, so Eastman bought a camera. The camera was a large, unwieldy box, which had to be mounted on a heavy tripod and instead of film there were individual glass plates that had to be coated with light-sensitive emulsion in situ and held in large plate holders. For outdoor shooting, the plates had to be prepared in a portable tent that doubled as a darkroom.

In 1878, Eastman read about "dry plates", invented in 1871 by the English photographer Richard Leach Maddox. The emulsion was sealed onto the plates with gelatine. These plates could be stored then used whenever desired, making obsolete much of the equipment Eastman had bought. While he was still working at the bank, Eastman devoted all his spare time to finding the perfect way to mass-produce dry plates.

In 1880, Eastman set up the Eastman Dry Plate Company. He began making and selling dry plates in 1881, and soon realized that glass could be replaced by a lighter, flexible material. In 1884, he had the idea of making the flexible plate into a roll. A roll holder could be mounted in place of the plate holder inside the camera. His first camera to feature a roll of film, dubbed the "detective camera", became available in 1885. The roll was made of paper, but this was far from ideal since the grain of the paper showed up on the prints. Meanwhile, other people were working on flexible dry plates, too. Several were

LEFT: *Dry plate camera, 1870s. Photography first took off with the advent of "wet plates" (1850) – glass slides coated in wet, light-sensitive solution. Dry plates were more convenient and afforded shorter exposure times; Eastman's first success was in mass-producing them.*

BELOW: *George Eastman using a 16-mme Cine-Kodak camera.*

BOTTOM LEFT: *The Eastman Dry Plate Company building, in Rochester, New York. Eastman moved to this building in 1883, after the commercial success of his dry plates. Today, Kodak's headquarters are situated at the same address, and the original building has been subsumed into the new.*

experimenting with a material called nitrocellulose, also known as celluloid. Eastman began selling celluloid film in 1889.

Eastman's real stroke of genius was his realization that, to be successful, he would need to expand the market for photography, and that would mean, in Eastman's own words, making photography "as convenient as a pencil". To do that, he had to invent a new, smaller, affordable camera. In 1888, the first Kodak camera went on sale. It was an immediate success.

The camera came loaded with a roll able to record 100 photographs. Once a camera's owner had taken the pictures, he or she had only to send the camera to Eastman's company and wait for the pictures and the return of the camera, newly loaded with film. The key to the Kodak's success was changing the perception of photography to something that anyone could do. Eastman had a simple phrase that did just that: "You press the button, we do the rest."

Eastman changed the name of his company to Eastman Kodak, and cornered the market in affordable photography. He never married, nor did he have any children. He was a great philanthropist, giving away large sums of money to universities, hospitals and dental clinics. His last two years were painful as he was suffering from a degenerative bone disease and he took his own life in 1932 by shooting himself in the heart. His suicide note read: "My work is done; why wait?".

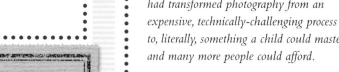

ABOVE: *Girl taking a picture with a Kodak Brownie camera, 1900s. Within a few years, Eastman's Brownie cameras had transformed photography from an expensive, technically-challenging process to, literally, something a child could master and many more people could afford.*

BELOW: *After its introduction to still photography in 1925, 35mm roll film (left) dominated the market in affordable photography until the introduction of consumer digital cameras in the 1990s. At the heart of a digital camera is a charge coupled device (CCD, right). On the surface of this semiconductor chip are millions of light-sensitive units; each one stores and releases an amount of charge that depends upon the intensity of light that falls on it, and a computer translates those charges into digital information.*

THE BROWNIE

The first camera with mass-market appeal, the Kodak, retailed at $25 (5 shillings in the UK). This was only half what Eastman paid for the first camera he bought, but it was still prohibitively expensive for everyday photography. In 1900, the Eastman Kodak Company introduced the first of its most successful range of cameras: the Brownie. Eastman Kodak made and sold 99 different models of Brownies between 1900 and 1980.

The first Brownie was a cardboard box that contained a roll holder, a roll of film and a lens. On the outside, there was a shutter button and a spool winder. The epitome of simplicity, it sold for just $1 (equivalent to about $20 in 2010), and brought in the era of the "snapshot" – a photograph taken without preparation that can capture a moment in time which would otherwise be lost.

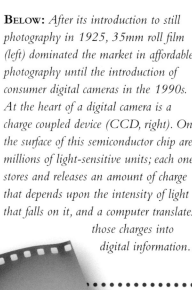

NIKOLA TESLA

(10 JULY 1856–7 JANUARY 1943)

SERBIAN-AMERICAN GENIUS NIKOLA TESLA WOULD BE VERY MUCH AT HOME IN TODAY'S DEVELOPED WORLD, WITH ITS ALMOST UBIQUITOUS ELECTRICITY SUPPLY AND ITS WIDESPREAD RELIANCE ON WIRELESS TECHNOLOGIES. HIS VISION AND DETERMINATION WENT A LONG WAY TOWARDS CREATING IT.

Nikola Tesla was born into a Serbian family in Smiljan, now in the Republic of Croatia but at the time of his birth part of the Austrian Empire. He studied engineering, first in Austria then in Prague, where he had to drop out after only a few months because his father died. Nevertheless, in 1880, he landed a job as a telephone engineer in Budapest.

In 1882, Telsa had a flash of inspiration that resulted in one of his most important inventions: the AC (alternating current) motor. AC is electric current that repeatedly changes the direction it flows along a wire, unlike DC (direct current), which flows in one direction only. Inside Tesla's motor, AC passes through a clever arrangement of coils, producing a rotating magnetic field that spins the rotor (the rotating part). Also in 1882, American inventor Thomas Edison (1847–1931) opened the world's first steam-driven power-generating stations, one in London and one in New York; both produced DC, which Edison favoured because no AC motors were available, and Edison's light bulbs – the main reason for generating power at the time – did not work well with AC.

Tesla worked for a year for an Edison subsidiary in France, and in 1884 he moved to America. All he had was 4 cents and a letter of recommendation from his boss to Edison himself. Edison gave Tesla a job, and promised him $50,000 if he could improve on Edison's DC generators. Within a year, Tesla had succeeded, but Edison was not forthcoming with the money. Tesla asked for a raise instead, but was again refused, and he resigned.

ABOVE: *A demonstration model made by Tesla of an induction motor – perhaps Tesla's most important invention – stripped down to show the coils of wire (stator) surrounding the rotor. Alternating current in the stator creates a rotating magnetic field, which pulls the rotor around.*

BOTTOM LEFT: *Tesla in his Colorado Springs laboratory. To the left is his "magnifying transmitter", which could produce millions of volts. The meandering sparks stretch about 7 metres (23 feet) across the laboratory. The photograph was probably a double exposure – with Tesla in one and the sparks in another.*

LEFT: *Sparks of "artificial lightning" fly from a large tesla coil, Nemesis, built by the Tesla Coil Builders Association, in the USA. Nemesis runs on mains voltage (110 volts in the USA), but produces more than a million volts.*

During the months that followed, Tesla developed a power distribution system based on AC; he took out several patents in 1887. Alternating current power distribution is cheaper to install, more efficient and more versatile than DC systems. American inventor George Westinghouse (1846–1914) was impressed with Tesla's ideas, and in 1888 he gave Tesla a job. There ensued a battle between Edison (DC) and Westinghouse (AC), but Tesla's system won out, and his AC motor has driven the wheels of industry ever since.

Around this time, Tesla hit upon two ideas that were to dominate his thinking from then on: the first was the transmission of electric power without wires; the second was wireless transmission of information (radio). In 1889, Tesla began experimenting with very high-voltage, high-frequency AC (current that oscillates thousands of times every second). Around 1891, he invented the Tesla coil: a kind of transformer that can produce very high voltages. Initially designed to provide wireless power to lights, it played an important role in the development of radio, television and X-ray technology. Meanwhile, Tesla continued his research into wireless broadcasting. Several other inventors were working on the same idea, but Tesla's mastery of high-frequency electricity put him ahead. In 1898, he designed and built the first remotely controlled vehicle: a boat, which he demonstrated to an amazed crowd in Madison Square Garden, New York.

In 1901, on Long Island, New York, work began on Wardenclyffe Tower, a hugely ambitious project Tesla hoped would demonstrate the potential for transmitting energy and information worldwide. Even as work was beginning on Tesla's tower, the Italian inventor Guglielmo Marconi (1874–1937) transmitted a radio signal across the Atlantic Ocean. The US Patent Office awarded priority in the invention of radio to Marconi. In 1905, funding for Tesla's project dried up, and the project was shut down.

His patents lapsed, and with no financial backing, Tesla declared himself bankrupt in 1916 and spent the rest of his life in relative poverty and increasing obscurity. A few months after his death, however, the US Supreme Court overturned the earlier decision, and named Tesla as the real inventor of radio.

RIGHT: *Wardenclyffe Tower, 57 metres (187 feet) high, with metal pipes pushing 125 metres (400 feet) into the ground. Tesla hoped that electrical oscillations would "shake" the earth and travel through the atmosphere, enabling the worldwide broadcasts of sound and pictures.*

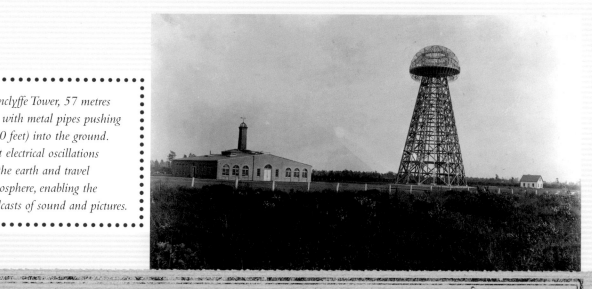

WAR OF CURRENTS

Nikola Tesla's most important achievement is his design of the power distribution system that has become the standard way of delivering electrical power from generator to consumer. Based on alternating currents, it superseded Thomas Edison's direct current system.

In 1893, the superiority of Tesla's AC system became apparent when the Westinghouse Electrical Company provided impressive electrification of the Chicago World's Fair. That same year, Tesla had the chance to fulfil a childhood dream: to harness the power of the Niagara Falls. He and Westinghouse (right) won the contract to build a power plant there, and their success when the first electricity flowed in 1896 did much to bolster the cause of AC power systems. In the years that followed, Edison mounted a bitter publicity campaign denouncing AC as dangerous, even going so far as orchestrating public electrocutions of animals and being involved in the development of the first electric chair (which was AC). Despite the campaign, the advantages of Tesla's system guaranteed its success.

AUGUSTE AND LOUIS LUMIÈRE

(19 OCTOBER 1862–10 APRIL 1954 AND 5 OCTOBER 1864–6 JUNE 1948)

WHILE NO SINGLE PERSON CAN BE CREDITED WITH INVENTING MOVING PICTURES, TWO FRENCH BROTHERS, AUGUSTE AND LOUIS LUMIÈRE, STAND OUT FOR THEIR FORESIGHT AND THEIR IMPORTANT CONTRIBUTIONS. USING A FILM CAMERA-PROJECTOR THAT THEY DESIGNED, THEY PUT ON SOME OF THE EARLIEST PUBLIC FILM SCREENINGS AND HELPED TO DEFINE CINEMA.

Auguste and Louis Lumière were born in Besançon, France, where their father Antoine had a photographic studio. In 1870, they moved to Lyon, and their father opened a small factory that made photographic plates. In 1882, Auguste and Louis helped to bring the factory back from the brink of financial collapse by mechanizing the production of the plates, and by selling a new type of plate that Louis had invented the previous year. The firm moved to a larger factory in Montplaisir, on the outskirts of Lyon, where it employed 300 people.

In 1894, the brothers' father attended a demonstration of the Kinetoscope, a moving picture peep-show device developed at the laboratory of American inventor Thomas Edison (1847–1931). The Kinetoscope was not a projector – only one person could watch a film at a time – but it was fast becoming popular entertainment. Antoine saw a commercial opportunity and, returning to Lyon, suggested his sons work on producing an apparatus that could record and play back moving images.

Louis, the more technically minded of the two brothers, designed the camera-projector, while Auguste designed the housing for the light source. Louis developed the film transport mechanism, inspired by a similar device in sewing machines, which allowed each frame of the film to stop momentarily behind the lens.

The Lumière brothers patented their camera-projector, the Cinématographe, in February 1895. Louis shot their first film, which was called *La Sortie de l'Usine Lumière à Lyon* (*Workers Leaving the Lumière Factory in Lyon*), and the pair showed the film to the Société d'Encouragement de l'Industrie Nationale, in Paris in March 1895, the first public screening of a film.

After several other screenings in France, their father arranged for the first performances to a paying audience. Ten films were shown 20 times a day. The opening night, at the Salon Indien – the empty basement of the Grand Café in Paris – was in December 1895. Auguste and Louis did not attend the first day, because they felt the technology still needed more work.

ABOVE: *One frame from the Lumière Brothers' first film,* La Sortie de l'Usine Lumière à Lyon, *1895. The film was shot at 16 frames per second and, at that rate, it runs for just under 50 seconds. It features most of the nearly 300 workers – mostly women – walking or cycling out of the factory yard.*

BELOW: *The Lumière Cinématographe – an all-in-one film camera, printer and projector. For shooting, only the camera is needed: the wooden box. The magic-lantern lamphouse – the large black box – contains the light source for projection. The film holder can be seen protruding from the camera-projector box.*

LEFT: *Auguste (looking down the microscope) and Louis Lumière in Auguste's laboratory, 1930s.*

After a slow start, the shows became a great success. In 1896, the Lumière brothers sent their agents abroad, demonstrating their Cinématographe and arousing great interest. They also ordered 200 or so of the camera-projectors to be constructed, and opened agencies in several countries to sell them. The Lumière franchise was very successful, but they refused to sell their devices to anyone except through their own agents.

By 1897, Thomas Edison had developed a system of sprocket holes that was incompatible with the Cinématographe and that was quickly becoming the standard in a rapidly developing industry. By 1905, Edison's system would predominate and the Lumière brothers would leave the film business.

Auguste's interests turned to chemistry and medicine. In 1910, he founded a laboratory in Lyon, where his 150 staff carried out research into cancer and other diseases. Auguste invented a dressing for burns, called *tulle gras*, which is still used today, and pioneered the use of film in surgery, which helped generations of medical students. Meanwhile, in the early 1900s, Louis demonstrated a sequence shot on a new, wider-format film, and later experimented with panoramic and stereoscopic (3-D) films.

In 1904, the Lumière brothers perfected a colour photography system called Autochrome; they had been working on colour photography since the early 1890s. Autochrome was the most important colour photographic process until colour film became available in the 1930s.

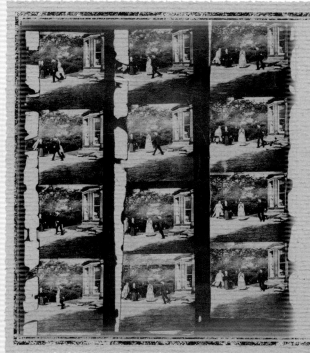

PIONEERS OF MOTION PICTURES

The Lumière brothers may have pioneered cinema, but they were not the first to make moving-picture films. Many inventors, scientists and photographers were experimenting with moving pictures several years before the Lumières. One of the first people to capture realistic movement on film was French inventor Louis Le Prince (1841–1890). Le Prince made his first successful film in October 1888. This was a sequence shot in his father-in-law's garden at Roundhay in Leeds, England, showing his son, his in-laws and a family friend.

The Lumières were not the first to project films to a paying audience, either. Projection and a paying audience form the definition of cinema. That honour of the first cinema performance goes to American brothers Grey and Otway Latham, who projected their films in New York in May 1895. But the "projector" they were using was simply a modified Edison Kinetoscope, and the results were not very good.

WILBUR AND ORVILLE WRIGHT

(16 APRIL 1867–30 MAY 1912 AND 19 AUGUST 1871–30 JANUARY 1948)

AT THE DAWN OF THE TWENTIETH CENTURY, TWO BROTHERS FROM A SMALL TOWN IN THE USA — WILBUR AND ORVILLE WRIGHT — BECAME THE FIRST TO ACHIEVE SUSTAINED, POWERED FLIGHT.

The key to their success was the combination of their inventive, mechanical skill with the application of scientific principles to flight. Moreover, they learned to become pilots in a gradual, thoughtful way, rather than risking everything on one short trial, like so many other pioneers.

Wilbur (seen right) and Orville (left) Wright grew up in Dayton, Ohio, in a family with seven children (although two died in childhood). They were mechanically-minded from an early age: in 1886, they built their own lathe; in 1888, they built a printing press, which they used to produce their own local paper; and in 1892, they opened a bicycle repair shop. They used the profits of the shop to finance their efforts in aviation.

The dream of human flight stretches back to antiquity, but it was only in the late eighteenth century that people finally made it into the air, by courtesy of "lighter-than-air" balloons. In the nineteenth century, scientists and inventors began giving serious consideration to the problem of "heavier-than-air" flight. Providing power was problematic, since steam engines were large and very heavy. During the 1880s and 1890s people flew in unpowered gliders and kites. In 1899, the Wright brothers built a large box kite. Wilbur hit on the idea that by twisting the box shape, it would be possible to change the airflow over the wings and make the kite bank and turn. He called this "wing warping", and it would be crucial to the brothers' later success.

After the kite performed well, the brothers decided to build full-size, piloted gliders, with wing warping effected via control cables. They constructed their first glider in 1900, and also added a front "wing" called an elevator, for pitch control. They chose the open area on the coast, near the tiny fishing village of Kitty Hawk in North Carolina, for its steady on-shore winds. First they flew the glider tethered like a kite, moving to the nearby Kill Devil Hills for actual flights. During 1901 and 1902, Wilbur and Orville built and tested two more gliders, and they also carried out hundreds of experiments in a homemade wind tunnel in their bicycle shop back in Dayton. By analysis and practical trials the brothers became the first to realize that controlling an aircraft required the banking control (wing warping or aileron), rudder and elevator all to be used continuously in combination. They were now ready to make a powered version of their flying machine.

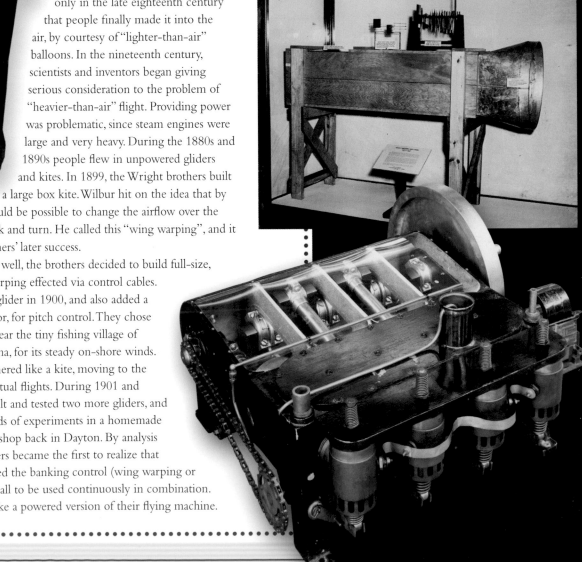

BELOW: *The Wright brothers' wind tunnel, which they built in their bicycle workshop in Dayton, Ohio. They used the wind tunnel to test wing designs — in particular the appropriate wing camber — to compile the first accurate tables of lift and drag forces on wings and understand how the lift force moves back or forward as the wing tilts, affecting control.*

BOTTOM: *Replica of the engine that powered the Wright Flyer. The engine was built in 1903 by Wilbur and Orville's bicycle-shop mechanic, Charlie Taylor (1868–1956). It was relatively light, thanks to the fact that the cylinder block was cast in aluminium.*

For driving the aeroplane, they designed and built large wooden propellers and, with a colleague in the bicycle shop, made a purpose-built, lightweight, powerful engine.

In December 1903, at Kill Devil Hills, the Wright brothers were ready to put all their ideas, experiments and calculations to the test. The first successful flights took place on December 17. There were four flights that day, two by each brother. The first, with Orville piloting, lasted just 12 seconds and covered 37 metres (120 feet). The final flight of the day, with Wilbur as pilot, lasted 59 seconds and covered 260 metres (852 feet). By 1905, the Wright brothers' flying machines were routinely staying in the air for several minutes at a time, taking off, landing, and manouevering with ease. At first, the world was slow to recognize the Wrights' achievement, despite the fact that there were several witnesses on the day. This was partly because the media and the public were unwilling to believe that the age-old dream of flight had finally come true, but also because

ABOVE: *The Wright Flyer's first flight. Orville is piloting (lying down, to reduce drag), Wilbur beside the wing tip. The rudders are at the rear, as are the two counter-rotating propellers, which are blurred out. The Flyer was launched from a wooden track.*

the brothers became secretive about their work, hoping to sell their invention to a government or large corporation.

Wilbur and Orville were awarded a patent in 1906, for a "Flying Machine". Three years later they founded The Wright Company, to take advantage of the patent. Unfortunately, Wilbur died within three years, from typhoid. Orville went on to become a long-time advisor to the US Government's National Advisory Committee for Aeronautics, and was able to appreciate the incredibly rapid developments in aviation that took place within a few decades of those first flights.

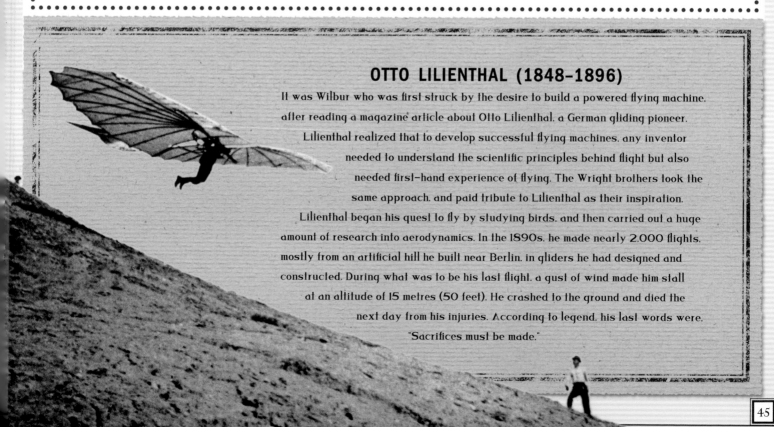

OTTO LILIENTHAL (1848–1896)

It was Wilbur who was first struck by the desire to build a powered flying machine. after reading a magazine article about Otto Lilienthal. a German gliding pioneer. Lilienthal realized that to develop successful flying machines. any inventor needed to understand the scientific principles behind flight but also needed first-hand experience of flying. The Wright brothers took the same approach. and paid tribute to Lilienthal as their inspiration.

Lilienthal began his quest to fly by studying birds. and then carried out a huge amount of research into aerodynamics. In the 1890s. he made nearly 2,000 flights. mostly from an artificial hill he built near Berlin. in gliders he had designed and constructed. During what was to be his last flight. a gust of wind made him stall at an altitude of 15 metres (50 feet). He crashed to the ground and died the next day from his injuries. According to legend. his last words were.

"Sacrifices must be made."

GUGLIELMO MARCONI

(25 APRIL 1874–20 JULY 1937)

Tʜᴇ ᴇᴀʀʟʏ ʜɪsᴛᴏʀʏ ᴏғ ʀᴀᴅɪᴏ ɪs ᴄᴏᴍᴘʟᴇx, ᴀɴᴅ ᴄʀᴇᴅɪᴛ ɪs ᴅᴜᴇ ᴛᴏ ᴅᴏᴢᴇɴs ᴏғ ɪᴍᴘᴏʀᴛᴀɴᴛ ᴘɪᴏɴᴇᴇʀs. ᴏɴᴇ ᴏғ ᴛʜᴇ ᴍᴏsᴛ ɪᴍᴘᴏʀᴛᴀɴᴛ ᴀɴᴅ sᴜᴄᴄᴇssғᴜʟ ᴡᴀs ɪᴛᴀʟɪᴀɴ ɪɴᴠᴇɴᴛᴏʀ Gᴜɢʟɪᴇʟᴍᴏ Mᴀʀᴄᴏɴɪ, ᴡʜᴏ ʜᴇʟᴘᴇᴅ ʙʀɪɴɢ ʀᴀᴅɪᴏ ɪɴᴛᴏ ᴇᴠᴇʀʏᴅᴀʏ ᴜsᴇ.

Guglielmo Marconi was born in Bologna, Italy to an Italian father and an Irish mother. From an early age, he took an interest in science and was particularly interested in electricity. In late 1894, Marconi became aware of the experiments of the German physicist Heinrich Hertz (1857–1894), who had succeeded in proving the existence of radio waves during the late 1880s.

Hertz produced radio waves by sending a rapidly alternating current up and down a vertical antenna, and detected the waves up to 20 metres (65 feet) away. Marconi also read about a demonstration that English physicist Oliver Lodge (1851–1940) had recently performed. Lodge sent Morse-code messages wirelessly, using the "Hertzian" waves. At the time, telegraph messages in Morse code could only be sent as electric pulses along wires, and Marconi was excited at the prospect of "wireless telegraphy".

Marconi decided to carry out experiments of his own, with the aim of making wireless telegraphy a useful, practical technology. He set up a laboratory in the attic room of his family home, and assembled the necessary components. He was soon sending and receiving Morse code wirelessly over increasingly large distances: first across the room, then down a corridor, then outside, across fields. In the summer of 1895, Marconi transmitted a message over nearly 2 kilometres (1.2 miles), and in 1896 patented his system. On being refused funding by the Italian government, he decided to travel to Britain to seek interest there.

Following a series of impressive demonstrations during 1897, Marconi garnered the support of the Post Office, which was in charge of Britain's telegraph system at the time. In that year, he formed the Wireless Telegraph & Signal Company to expand his work. In the following few years, he sent messages over ever greater distances and, notably, between ships and from ship to shore. In 1900, Marconi decided to try extending the range of his transmissions yet further: across the Atlantic Ocean. In 1901, he

Rɪɢʜᴛ: Sailors on board ship, reading a "marconigram", in the early 1900s. Just as a telegram was a physical record of a Morse code message sent via telegraph wires, a marconigram was a record – on paper tape – of Morse-code message received wirelessly via radio.

Lᴇғᴛ: Marconi in 1922, in the radio room of his yacht Elettra. Here he picked up radio signals he believed had come from planet Mars. In fact, they were probably "whistlers" – very low-frequency waves produced by lightning.

Aʙᴏᴠᴇ: Illustration of the receiving end of Marconi's first trans-Atlantic transmission in 1901. A kite was used to lift the antenna into the air at St Johns, Newfoundland, after a heavy storm destroyed the original fixed antenna at Cape Cod, Massachusetts.

created a worldwide sensation when he announced the successful transmission of a Morse code letter "S" (three short bursts of radio) from Poldhu, in Cornwall, England to St John's, Newfoundland (then a British colony, now in Canada). After suggestions that he had faked the transmission, he carried out another, carefully monitored experiment the following year. Aboard a ship close to the Canadian coast, he received signals from Cornwall more than 3,200 kilometres (2,000 miles) away.

During the years that followed, Marconi made several important improvements to his system of radio transmission, and in 1907 he instigated the first commercial trans-Atlantic radio service. He found fame again when the British ocean liner RMS *Titanic* hit an iceberg and sank in 1912. A Marconi-radio operator aboard the sinking ship managed to broadcast radio distress signals and summon help from nearby ships.

During the 1920s, Marconi experimented with much higher-frequency radio waves. These "short waves" can be focused by a curved reflector behind the transmitter, like the parabolic dishes used to receive satellite communications. This arrangement made radio more efficient and less power-hungry, since the waves were concentrated into a beam and not radiating in all directions. By this time, radio operators, including Marconi, were transmitting not only Morse code, but also speech, music and audio signals. In 1931, he experimented with even higher-frequency, shorter-wavelength radio waves – microwaves – and a year later, he installed a beamed, microwave radio-telephone system between the Vatican and the Pope's summer residence. Much of today's telecommunications infrastructure is built on microwave beams like this.

Marconi did not invent radio, but he did make several important improvements to it, and his determination to turn a complicated laboratory curiosity into something useful and commercially successful helped make the world feel a bit smaller. In 1909, he received the Nobel Prize for Physics, for his contributions to wireless telegraphy, and in 1930, he became president of the Royal Italian Academy.

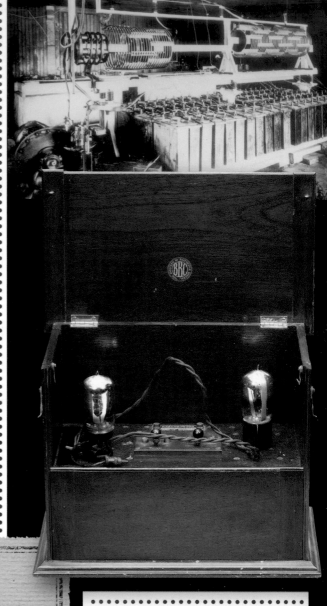

LEE DE FOREST
(1873-1961)

In the early 1900s, radio communication could only be made using wireless telegraphy – sending Morse-code messages as on-and-off pulses of radio waves. That changed with the introduction of audio broadcasting: regular broadcasts began in 1920. One of the most important technologies involved in the development of audio broadcasting was the Audion, invented in 1906 by American electronics engineer Lee de Forest.

The Audion was an early example of a "valve", which found myriad uses in the developing field of electronics. In radio and television broadcasting, it enabled the construction of all-electronic "oscillators", which produced radio waves of any frequency to order. From the 1920s until the 1960s, radio and television sets used valves for amplification. Eventually, they were replaced by the smaller, less power-hungry transistor, invented in 1947.

Top: *Batteries and tuning coils at Marconi's South Wellfleet station, Massachusetts. From here, in 1903, Marconi sent a message from US President Theodore Roosevelt to King Edward, in London – a distance of more than 5,000 kilometres (3,000 miles).*

Above: *"Marconiphone" amplifier from around 1925, with valves – the developments of de Forest's Audion (see box). Marconi formed the Marconiphone Company in 1922, to manufacture radios sets for domestic use as well as amplifiers like this one, which made it possible to listen without headphones.*

CARL BOSCH
(27 AUGUST 1874–26 APRIL 1940)

THERE IS ONE TWENTIETH- CENTURY INVENTION THAT ARGUABLY CHANGED THE WORLD MORE PROFOUNDLY THAN ANY OTHER. IT IS NOT A MACHINE OR A DEVICE, BUT AN INDUSTRIAL PROCESS. THE MANUFACTURE OF AMMONIA, PERFECTED BY GERMAN CHEMIST CARL BOSCH, ENABLED THE PRODUCTION OF FERTILIZERS AND EXPLOSIVES ON A COMPLETELY UNPRECEDENTED SCALE, RESULTING IN A METEORIC RISE IN POPULATION AND UNLIMITED EXPLOSIVE CAPACITY IN TWO WORLD WARS.

Carl Bosch was born in Cologne, Germany. He studied mechanical engineering and metallurgy at Charlottenburg Technical University. In 1896, he began studying chemistry, at the University of Leipzig. Three years later, Bosch joined Germany's most successful chemical company, in Ludwigshafen. At the time, the company's name was Badische Anilin- & Soda-Fabrik; nowadays, the name is simply BASF.

At first, Bosch worked on synthetic dyes, but in 1905 he turned his attention to a major question of the day: how to "fix" atmospheric nitrogen into chemical compounds. This seemingly esoteric issue was actually of immense global significance. Scientists in the nineteenth century had realized that nitrogen-rich compounds made very effective fertilizers. In particular, huge deposits of guano (fossilized bird excrement) and saltpetre (potassium nitrate, KNO_3) had helped to sustain an ever-expanding world population. In 1898, English chemist William Crookes (1832–1919) delivered a lecture to the British Association entitled "The Wheat Problem", in which he noted that these deposits were dwindling. Crookes suggested that the world could face major famines by the 1920s. In addition, nitrogen compounds were an essential ingredient in explosives. In the early years of the twentieth century, a growing threat of war led to further increases in the demand for nitrogen compounds.

As an element, nitrogen is notoriously unreactive. That is why it makes up nearly 80 per cent of the atmosphere. From the 1890s, chemists had tried in vain to find an efficient, high-yield process to fix nitrogen from the air to make fertilizers and explosives. Then, in 1905, German chemist Fritz Haber (1868–1934) reported that he had produced small amounts of ammonia from nitrogen gas (N_2) and hydrogen gas (H_2). Haber's process required high temperature, high pressure and a catalyst – a chemical that speeds up a reaction, while remaining unchanged, or a chemical that lowers the energy needed for a reaction to take place, therefore speeding it up. Haber was working under contract to BASF and, by 1909, he had produced an impressive yield of ammonia in his

BELOW: *A German World War I biplane dropping a bomb. At the time, the manufacture of explosives depended upon a plentiful source of nitrogen-rich compounds. Bosch's process for the manufacture of ammonia helped Germany meet the demand and sustain its war effort.*

ABOVE MIDDLE: *The world's first ammonia synthesis plant, at Oppau, near BASF's headquarters in Ludwigshafen, Germany. In its early years, the plant produced more than 7,000 tonnes of ammonia, made into 36,000 tonnes of ammonium sulphate. The four large towers are ammonia storage silos.*

ABOVE: *Synthetic ammonia fertilizer factory, 1920s. Before Bosch developed his industrial process, only bacteria, living in the soil or in water, could "fix" nitrogen from the air in these quantities. The production of synthetic nitrogen-based fertilizers enabled the world to avoid mass starvation.*

laboratory. In that year, BASF gave Bosch the task of scaling up Haber's reaction for use on an industrial scale.

Bosch developed a reaction vessel that could withstand the high temperatures and pressures that were necessary: a double-walled chamber that was safer and more efficient than Haber's system. He carried out nearly 20,000 experiments before he found a more suitable catalyst than the expensive osmium and uranium Haber had used. Bosch also worked out the best ways to obtain large quantities of hydrogen – by passing steam over red-hot coke – and nitrogen, from the air. He patented his results in 1910, and by 1911, BASF had begun producing ammonia in large quantities. The company opened the world's first dedicated ammonia plant, in Oppau, a suburb of Ludwigshafen, just two years later. The ammonia was used to make artificial fertilizers in huge quantities. When the First World War began in 1914, however, the German government was faced with a shortage of ammunition, and the output of the Oppau plant was used to produce explosives instead. Without the Haber-Bosch process, the war would probably not have lasted as long as it did; Britain had blockaded Germany's imports of saltpetre, which Germany had relied upon to make explosives.

Bosch's intensive work and his insight into chemistry and engineering helped to lay the foundations of large-scale, high-pressure processes – which, in turn, underpin much of the modern chemical industry. In 1931, he was awarded the Nobel Prize for Chemistry. Today, nearly 200 million tonnes of synthetic nitrogen fertilizers are produced worldwide every year – several tonnes every second – using the Haber-Bosch process.

ABOVE: *German chemist Fritz Haber, photographed in 1918, the year he won the Nobel Prize for Chemistry. Haber developed the reaction that produces ammonia from nitrogen and hydrogen gases, which Bosch successfully scaled up in 1910; the resulting technique is today called the Haber-Bosch Process.*

LEFT: *A tractor spraying nitrogen-rich artificial fertilizers on a rice paddy field in Spain. In the twentieth century, the availability of artificial fertilizers and the mechanization of farming equipment led to the rise of intensive agriculture, a system with high-energy input and dramatically increased crop yields.*

FERTILIZERS

Carl Bosch made it possible to produce huge quantities of ammonia, much of which is made into nitrogen-rich ammonium nitrate (NH_4NO_3) fertilizer. Careful estimates suggest that synthetic fertilizers feed about half of the world's population. Plants rely upon nitrogen compounds for building proteins and DNA (deoxyribonucleic acid). In nature, nitrates come from decaying plant and animal matter and from certain bacteria, which fix nitrogen from the air.

Bosch's lasting legacy is double-edged, however. Artificial fertilizers have saved millions from starvation, but the huge increases in population they allowed, from nearly 1.8 billion in 1910 to nearly 7 billion a century later, have put a strain on the world's resources. Their manufacture accounts for about one per cent of the world's total energy consumption and their use causes pollution: agricultural run-off in particular creates "harmful algal blooms" in lakes and estuaries due to the extra nitrogen.

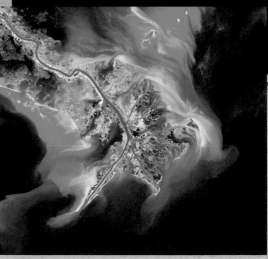

ABOVE: *The heavy use of artificial fertilizers causes dead zones, like this one in the Gulf of Mexico. Dead zones form in lakes and coastal seas as agricultural run-off finds its way into water courses, causing a proliferation of algae (as a result of the extra nitrogen), which starve other organisms of oxygen.*

VLADIMIR ZWORYKIN

(30 JULY 1889–29 JULY 1982)

TELEVISION CHANGED THE WAY OF LIFE OF HUNDREDS OF MILLIONS OF PEOPLE IN THE TWENTIETH CENTURY. BUT THE HISTORY OF THIS FAR-REACHING INVENTION IS FAR FROM SIMPLE: DOZENS OF INVENTIVE PEOPLE CONTRIBUTED TO ITS DEVELOPMENT. ONE OF THE MOST SIGNIFICANT PIONEERS WAS RUSSIAN-BORN INVENTOR VLADIMIR ZWORYKIN, WHO ALSO MADE IMPORTANT CONTRIBUTIONS TO THE DEVELOPMENT OF THE ELECTRON MICROSCOPE.

Vladimir Zworykin was born in the town of Murom, in what was then the Russian Empire. As a child he spent time installing and repairing electric doorbells in the family-owned passenger steamships. In 1912, he obtained a degree in engineering from the Saint Petersburg Institute of Technology. At the Institute, one of Zworykin's professors, Boris Rosing (1869–1933) showed him a project he had

ABOVE: *Vladimir Zworykin holding an early vacuum tube. Zworykin invented the iconoscope, an early camera tube, and the kinescope, an early television display – both vacuum tubes, and both very important in the development of television.*

TOP RIGHT: *Combined electronic television set and radio receiver, 1938, made by British company Pye. The 23-centimetre (9-inch) cathode ray tube (CRT) screen is a descendant of Zworykin's kinescope, the first practical television display..*

TELEVISION PIONEERS

For much of the 1930s, Vladimir Zworykin was embroiled in a lengthy patent battle between the Radio Corporation of America (RCA) and another television pioneer, American inventor Philo T Farnsworth (1906–1971). Farnsworth won the battle – at great cost to RCA. Another important figure in developing electronic television was Hungarian inventor Kálmán Tihanyi (1897–1947), whose work was crucial in making Zworykin's Iconoscope camera work. There was another approach to television besides the all-electronic system: the "electromechanical system". In 1924, Scottish inventor John Logie Baird (1888–1946; shown above, standing by the railings) transmitted the first-ever television pictures. The earliest photograph of a television picture (left) shows Baird's business partner. Instead of electron beams scanning the inside of a cathode ray tube, Baird's device used spinning discs with spiral holes to produce images. Electromechanical systems made some of the earliest television broadcasts – but electronic television won out in the end.

been working on in secret. Rosing called it "electric telescopy" – one of the early names for television; several other people in other countries were working on the same idea.

Indeed, as early as 1908 the Scottish engineer AA Campbell Swinton (1863–1930) had published a letter in which he outlined his concept for "distant electric vision" using the cathode-ray tube, invented in 1897 by German physicist Karl Ferdinand Braun (1850–1918). A cathode-ray tube is a glass tube, from which the air has been removed, in which a beam of electrons strikes a flat screen. The inside of the screen is coated with chemical compounds called phosphors, which glow wherever electrons collide with them. Electromagnets positioned around the tube control the direction of the beam, and the television signal fed to the magnets causes the beam to scan in horizontal lines across the screen. By scanning the whole screen in this way several times every second, while also varying the intensity of the electron beam, it is possible to display a moving image. Swinton never attempted to build the system he conceived, and while Rosing was a pioneer, his system was crude and unwieldy, and never worked.

In 1919, after the Bolshevik Revolution during the Russian Civil War, Zworykin emigrated to the USA. Within a year he had begun working at the Westinghouse Electric and Manufacturing Company in Pittsburgh. In 1923, after spending a considerable amount of his spare time working on television, he applied for a patent. Zworykin's system used one cathode-ray tube to display pictures and another one in the camera. Inside his television camera, light fell on the screen of the cathode-ray tube. Instead of phosphors, this screen was coated with light-sensitive dots made of potassium hydride. An electron beam scanned the screen, as in the picture tube, and each light-sensitive dot produced a signal that depended on the brightness of the image at that point.

After submitting an improved patent application in 1925, Zworykin demonstrated his television system to his employers at Westinghouse. The images were dim and stationary, and his employers were not impressed.

ABOVE: *Zworykin standing next to an early scanning electron microscope, around 1945. Zworykin did not invent the electron microscope, but he led a team that made important improvements in the device, which has revolutionized biology, medicine and materials science.*

LEFT: *Zworykin's night-vision device, the snooperscope, photographed in 1944. The snooperscope was sensitive to infrared radiation – or "heat rays" – which warm-blooded animals (including humans) emit with greater intensity than non-living things, by virtue of their warm bodies. Zworykin's device helped soldiers in night-time conflicts during World War II.*

He received a more favourable response when he showed it to the Radio Corporation of America (RCA) in 1929. Zworykin's camera, later dubbed the Iconoscope, would become the standard way of producing television pictures. Zworykin developed the technology further at the RCA. In 1939, the company demonstrated it at the New York World's Fair and, in 1941, the RCA began regular commercial television broadcasts in the USA.

Zworykin's work on the electron microscope stemmed from his wealth of experience working with images and electrons. In 1938, he employed Canadian electronic engineer James Hillier (1915–2007) and worked with him to improve on the electron microscope, which had been invented in the early 1930s in Germany. In particular, the team developed the scanning electron microscope, in which a beam of electrons scans a sample – not unlike what happens inside a cathode-ray tube. In 1940, Zworykin's team achieved the first magnification greater than 100,000x – a huge improvement in the technology.

In addition to his work in television and electron microscopy, Zworykin developed infrared "night vision", missile guidance systems and security systems that used "electric eyes". He received a total of 120 US patents.

JUAN DE LA CIERVA

(21 September 1895–9 December 1935)

A STRANGE AIRCRAFT TOOK TO THE AIR IN 1923. IT WAS THE AUTOGYRO, AN AEROPLANE WITH BOTH A PROPELLER AND A ROTOR, INVENTED BY SPANISH ENGINEER JUAN DE LA CIERVA. TODAY, THE AUTOGYRO IS ONLY FLOWN BY ENTHUSIASTS, HAVING BEEN SUPERSEDED BY THE MORE MANOEUVRABLE HELICOPTER. THE MOST IMPORTANT FEATURE OF HELICOPTER DESIGN, HOWEVER, THE COMPLICATED MECHANICS AT THE HUB OF THE ROTOR, WAS ESTABLISHED IN CIERVA'S AUTOGYROS.

Juan de la Cierva was born to a wealthy family in Mercia, Spain. As a boy, he was inspired by the early pioneers of flight, and he became determined to be an aviator himself. In 1911, he went to study civil engineering in Madrid. That year, he and two friends experimented with gliders, and formed an aviation company. In 1912, Cierva built the first aeroplane in Spain, but during the following few years two of his aeroplanes crashed after stalling at low speed. As a result, he became determined to build an aeroplane that could not stall. He came up with the autogyro: an aeroplane

with a propeller at the front and rotating wings – rotor blades – at the top. The rotor blades would always be moving fast relative to the air, and producing lift, even when the autogyro was moving slowly.

Other inventors had experimented with rotors as early as 1907, but with little success. Cierva decided to leave his rotors unpowered, so that they would windmill or "autorotate" as the autogyro moved through the air. This approach had an added benefit: if the engine cut out, the autogyro would not crash to the ground. Instead, it would fall slowly, like a spinning sycamore seed case. In 1920, Cierva patented his idea, and tested small models of his autogyro concept. The models worked well, but when he scaled up his design, he found it had a tendency to flip over. He soon realized why. As it turns, each rotor blade spends half the time moving forwards – into the oncoming air – and half the time moving backwards. This means that the advancing blade is moving through the air faster than the receding blade and so the lift force is greater on one side than the other.

Cierva looked back at his earlier models, and realized that the smaller

ABOVE: *Juan de la Cierva (in front, piloting) in his C8 autogyro in September 1928, just before leaving Croydon Airfield, UK, en route to Paris, France. In Cierva's company's name, "Autogiro" was spelt with an "i", while the generic name for this kind of rotary-wing craft was "autogyro".*

LEFT: *A Cierva autogyro taking off from the South Grounds of the White House in Washington, DC, in 1931. The aircraft has fixed wings, like an aeroplane, but most of the lift force is provided by the rotor blades. In 1933, Cierva dispensed with the fixed wings altogether.*

BELOW: *A modern, fully articulated rotor. Each blade is able to move independently of the others, and can tilt to increase or decrease the lift force. Cierva developed the fully articulated rotor so that he could control his autogyros without fixed wings.*

rotor blades were flexible. As those rotors turned, the blades twisted slightly, automatically adjusting to the changing airspeed during each rotation, and producing constant lift. Cierva set about mimicking this phenomenon in his larger, metal blades. To do this, he incorporated a "flapping hinge" where each rotor blade met the rotor hub. In January 1923, Cierva's first successful prototype, the C4, flew 180 metres (200 yards) at an airfield near Madrid. This was the first stable flight of a rotating-wing aircraft in history, and was quickly followed by many longer, more sustained flights. In 1925, Cierva demonstrated autogyro C6 in England and, with the support of an investor, formed the Cierva Autogiro Company. Three years later, Cierva flew his C8 autogyro from England to France. The C8 featured a "fully articulated rotor", with blades that could flex backwards to absorb the drag force (air resistance), which had previously caused some blades to snap.

More improvements followed, including a system to drive the rotor, just at take-off, so that the autogyro could rise vertically. The most obvious change came in 1933 when Cierva built autogyros with no wings and no tail. Up to this point, autogyros were controlled in the same way as fixed-wing aircraft: using moveable flaps on the wings and tail. This meant that pilots all but lost control at low speeds, so Cierva decided to find a way to control his autogyros by tilting the rotor. To do this, he had to design a complicated system of hinges and control levers around his rotor hub, and what he achieved formed the basis of all future helicopter rotors. Ironically, after devoting his career to avoiding the problems of stalling, Cierva was killed at Croydon airport, a passenger aboard a conventional fixed-wing aeroplane that stalled and crashed into a building just after take-off.

ABOVE: *A Focke-Wulf Fw-61, the first fully controllable helicopter, in 1937. German engineer Heinrich Focke (1890–1979) designed this after working on Cierva autogyros. The pilot is German aviator Hanna Reitsch (1912–1979), who set many records, including being the first woman to fly helicopters.*

BELOW: *Russian-American helicopter pioneer Igor Sigorsky, flying his VS-300 helicopter in 1940. The VS-300 was the first helicopter to have a tail rotor; until then, helicopters had two counter-rotating main rotors to keep them stable in flight. Both designs are still common today.*

HELICOPTERS

The autogyro, invented by Juan de la Cierva and later developed by Russian engineer Igor Bensen (1917–2000), was effective, safe, and moved through the air almost as fast as some aeroplanes. Autogyros found several uses during the Second World War, including reconnaissance and even the bombing of submarines. But autogyros could not hover, or perform truly vertical landings and take-offs so eventually helicopters gained the edge once they became practical.

It was Russian-American aviation pioneer Igor Sikorsky (1889–1972) who established the blueprint for the modern helicopter. Sikorsky built his first helicopter in 1909 but, as with other inventors' attempts at the time, it did not work. After working on fixed-wing aircraft during the 1910s and '20s, Sikorsky eventually produced one of the world's first successful helicopters, the VS-300, in 1939. He went on to design the first mass-produced helicopter, the Sikorsky R-4, in 1942. The overall layout of most helicopters has changed little since then.

WERNHER VON BRAUN
(23 MARCH 1912–16 JUNE 1977)

GERMAN-AMERICAN ROCKET ENGINEER WERNHER VON BRAUN DESIGNED THE FIRST ROCKET-POWERED LONG-RANGE BALLISTIC MISSILES — BUT HIS REAL ACHIEVEMENT WAS IN SPACEFLIGHT. HIS DETERMINATION IN FOLLOWING HIS BOYHOOD DREAM OF SENDING PEOPLE TO THE MOON, TOGETHER WITH HIS EXCELLENT TECHNICAL AND LEADERSHIP SKILLS, MADE HIM THE ULTIMATE SPACEFLIGHT PIONEER OF THE TWENTIETH CENTURY.

Wernher von Braun was born a baron, to an aristocratic family in the town of Wirsitz, in the then German Empire (now Wyrzysk in Poland). After the First World War, his family moved to Berlin, Germany. Young Wernher became interested in space when his mother, a serious amateur astronomer, gave him a telescope – and he was mesmerized by stories of journeys into outer space. Von Braun studied mechanical engineering at the Charlottenburg Institute of Technology, in Berlin. While there, he joined the Verein für Raumschiffahrt (VfR) – the Society for Spaceship Travel – and became involved in building and firing early liquid-fuel rockets.

Von Braun joined the German army's Ordnance Division in October 1932, developing and testing rockets at an artillery range in Kummersdorf, near Berlin. He became technical head of the "Aggregate" programme, whose main aim was to design rockets for use as long-range ballistic missiles. In 1935, von Braun's team moved to Peenemünde, on the Baltic Coast, where the programme continued until the end of the Second World War, in 1945. Each rocket in the proposed Aggregate series was bigger and more ambitious than the last. For

BELOW: *An A-4 rocket on a test launch at Peenemünde, Germany, in 1943. The A-4 became the V-2 when used during World War II. Payload: 1 tonne; maximum altitude: 95 kilometres (50 miles); maximum speed: 5,800 kilometres per hour (3,600 miles per hour); range: 320 kilometres (199 miles).*

RIGHT: *Officials of the US Army Ballistic Missile Agency at Redstone Arsenal in Huntsville, Alabama. Von Braun is second from right; in the foreground is Romanian rocket pioneer Hermann Oberth. The USA's first satellite, Explorer, was launched by a Jupiter-C rocket designed at ABMA.*

LEFT: *Wernher von Braun, in 1954, holding a model of a proposed rocket that would lift people into space. During the 1950s, von Braun was something of a celebrity in the USA, nurturing dreams of space travel among the postwar American people.*

example, the A9/10, had it ever been launched, would have been a 100-tonne, two-stage rocket aimed at New York, United States; the A12 would have been a true orbital launch vehicle, able to place satellites into orbit.

The only Aggregate rocket to see service was the A-4, better known as the V-2. Designed by von Braun's team, this was the world's first medium-range ballistic missile – and the first reliable liquid-fuel rocket. By the end of the war, more than 3,000 had been launched; these terrible weapons, built by prisoners-of-war, rained destruction upon England, Belgium and France from 1944 onwards. Von Braun's involvement in the weapon's development and his membership of the Nazi party remain controversial, but he was always preoccupied with his real goal of sending rockets into space. When the war ended, the US Army took von Braun and his team of workers to the United States. In 1950, von Braun settled in Huntsville, Alabama, where he headed the US Army rocket team. At that time, the Cold War was intensifying, and the United States was worried that the Soviet Union might dominate the new territory of space. Throughout the 1950s, von Braun became something of a celebrity, promoting the idea of space travel in books, magazines, on television and in films – inspiring the American people with his dreams of space stations and journeys to the Moon and Mars.

The Space Age officially began on 4 October 1957, when the Soviet Union launched the first satellite, Sputnik 1, into orbit. The news prompted the United States Government to form NASA (the National Aeronautics and Space Administration). In 1958, a Redstone rocket, designed by von Braun, put America's first satellite into orbit. Two years later, NASA opened its Marshall Spaceflight Center, in Huntsville, and von Braun became its director. The Soviet Union got the upper hand again in 1961, when it launched a human into space for the first time; the United States retaliated by launching Alan Shepherd into space less than a month later, again with a von Braun Redstone rocket.

In May 1961, to von Braun's delight, United States president John F Kennedy (1917–1963) announced the country's intention of "landing a man on the Moon and returning him back safely to the Earth". The United States succeeded – and the astronauts of the "Apollo" programme travelled to the Moon in modules launched into space atop huge Saturn V rockets, designed by von Braun's team at the Marshall Space Center. Von Braun had finally achieved his goal of interplanetary travel and NASA call him "without doubt, the greatest rocket engineer in history".

ABOVE: *The launch of the Apollo 11 mission, 16 July 1969, carried into space by a huge Saturn V rocket from Cape Kennedy, USA. This was the realization of a childhood ambition for von Braun, who led the project to design and build the Saturn V.*

LEFT: *Russian space visionary Konstantin Tsiolkovsky, whose 1903 book* The Exploration of Cosmic Space by Means of Reaction Devices *was the first serious scientific treatise on using rockets to reach space.*

EARLY SPACEFLIGHT PIONEERS

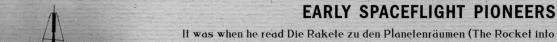

It was when he read Die Rakete zu den Planetenräumen (The Rocket into Interplanetary Space) that Wernher von Braun set about learning the mathematics, physics and engineering necessary to make space travel a reality. The book was written by German rocket pioneer Hermann Oberth (1894–1989), in 1923.

Oberth was one of three visionaries who independently worked out how multi-staged rockets could be used to lift into space. The other two were Russian mathematics teacher Konstantin Tsiolkovsky (1857–1935) and American physicist Robert Goddard (1882–1945). In 1926, Goddard became the first person to build and fly a liquid-fuel rocket, in his aunt's farm in Massachusetts. In his day, Goddard was ridiculed in the press. Nevertheless, Wernher von Braun, although himself an innovator, based much of his early work on Goddard's research.

ALAN TURING

T HE FIRST ELECTRONIC DIGITAL COMPUTERS APPEARED IN THE 1940S. THEY WERE NOT SIMPLY THE RESULT OF ADVANCES IN ELECTRONICS. THEIR DEVELOPMENT RELIED ON A THEORY OF COMPUTATION FORMULATED BY ENGLISH MATHEMATICIAN ALAN TURING, WHO WAS ALSO AN IMPORTANT WARTIME CODE-BREAKER AND A PIONEER OF MACHINE INTELLIGENCE.

Alan Turing was born in London to an upper-middle-class family, and his genius was evident from an early age. He taught himself to read in a matter of weeks and while in his teens at the auspicious Sherborne public school in Dorset he developed a fascination for science and mathematics. In 1931, he went to King's College, Cambridge, to study mathematics.

While he was at university, Turing became interested in logic. This was a hot topic in mathematics at the time: mathematicians were attempting to define their subject completely in terms of logic – to iron out inconsistencies and to show that mathematics is "logically complete". In 1931, German mathematician Kurt Gödel (1906–1978) had published two theorems that showed this was impossible. He proved that even simple mathematical statements rely on assumptions and intuition that cannot be defined in terms of logic.

Inspired by Gödel's theorems, Turing wrote a landmark paper on the logic of mathematics in 1936. In this paper, Turing imagined an "automatic machine" that could read and write symbols on a tape, and carry out tasks based on a simple set of instructions. Turing proved that any problem that is "computable" can be solved by such a machine – a "universal" computer – if given the correct set of instructions. This was another way of expressing Gödel's theorems, since it also proved there were some mathematical statements that the machine could not compute. It was significant for another reason: Turing's hypothetical device became known as the "Universal Turing Machine" and was to be the blueprint for digital computers.

During the Second World War, Turing worked for the UK

LEFT *The "keyboard" of the Z3, a computer built in 1941 by German engineer Konrad Zuse (1910–1995). The Z3 was the first "stored-program" computer to use binary to represent numbers and instructions.*

LEFT: *Alan Turing, photographed in 1951. No individual invented the computer, but Turing developed some fundamental theoretical and practical insights in the 1930s and '40s.*

BELOW: *A Colossus code-breaking computer at Bletchley Park, UK, 1943. Designed by English electronic engineer Tommy Flowers (1905–1998), the Colossus was the first fully electronic, stored-program computer – but it was not a truly general-purpose computer.*

LEFT: *Pilot ACE, 1950. Towards the end of World War II, Turing told his colleagues he was "building a brain": the Automatic Computing Engine (ACE). After the war, Turing presented his design to the National Physical Laboratory. Pilot ACE was the prototype based on Turing's design*

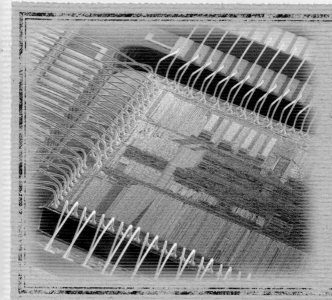

THE CENTRAL PROCESSING UNIT

A general-purpose computer is defined by the presence of a CPU (Central Processing Unit) to carry out instructions, memory to hold the instructions and some form of input and output. This basic architecture is called the von Neumann architecture, after Hungarian-American mathematician John von Neumann (1903–1957). In 1945, he presented a paper to the US Army proposing a general-purpose computing machine, with the ability to store programs. His proposal was based on the idea of the Universal Turing Machine developed by Turing. The computer was the EDVAC (Electronic Discrete Variable Automatic Computer), one of the earliest general-purpose computers, which ran its first programs in 1951. In modern computers, the CPU is contained on a chip of semiconductor called a microprocessor.

government helping to decode the German military forces' encrypted communications, at a Buckinghamshire mansion called Bletchley Park. The Germans used two devices, the Enigma machine and the Lorenz Cipher machine, to produce extremely well-encrypted communications. Although possible to find "keys" to crack the encryption, this was a laborious process. In the early 1930s, Polish code-breakers had built a machine that sped up the process. But in 1939, the Germans improved their machines, making the codes even harder to crack. Turing in turn designed a more efficient and faster machine, which he called "The Bombe". By the end of the war, 211 Bombes were operational, requiring 2,000 staff to run them. Turing's invention greatly helped the war effort, and probably shortened the war by a year or more.

After the war, he wrote a proposal to the National Physical Laboratory in London for an "automatic computing engine", based on his Universal Turing Machine. While his proposal was accepted, it was thought too ambitious, and a smaller version – the Pilot ACE – was built instead. It ran its first program in 1950. Other researchers were working on Turing Machines, too. The world's first stored-program, general-purpose computer was the Small Scale Experimental Machine, built by a team at the Victoria University of Manchester, also in England. It ran its first program in 1948.

Turing was well aware of the possibility that machines might one day "think". In an article in 1950, he suggested a test for artificial intelligence: a person (the judge) would have two conversations via a keyboard and monitor – one with a human being and one with a computer. If the judge was not certain which was which, the computer would be deemed intelligent. No computer has yet passed the test.

In 1945, Turing was awarded the OBE (Order of the British Empire) for his work at Bletchley Park, but in 1952 he was convicted for homosexuality, then illegal in the UK (the UK government issued a posthumous apology to Turing in 2009). Two years after his conviction, he was found dead in his bed from cyanide poisoning; an inquest concluded that it was suicide.

ABOVE: *ENLAC (Electronic Numerical Integrator and Computer), built by the US Army Ballistic Research Laboratory in 1946. The first general-purpose computing machine, designed to compute trajectories, its program was "stored" by physically manipulating switches and patch cables.*

LEFT: *John von Neumann, photographed in the 1940s. In his now-classic "First Draft of a Report on the EDVAC", von Neumann established the basic "architecture" of modern computers – although he was greatly inspired by ENIAC, which he had used in the development of the hydrogen bomb.*

GERTRUDE ELION

(23 JANUARY 1918–21 FEBRUARY 1999)

THE INVENTIONS OF AMERICAN BIOCHEMIST GERTRUDE ELION ARE FAR TOO SMALL TO SEE. THEY ARE WORKS OF ENGINEERING, BUT AT THE MOLECULAR LEVEL: ELION WAS A PIONEER OF CHEMOTHERAPY. THE MEDICINES SHE DEVELOPED HAVE BROUGHT HOPE TO MILLIONS OF PEOPLE WITH BACTERIAL AND VIRAL INFECTIONS AND CANCER.

Gertrude Elion was born in New York, USA. Her mother was from Russia, her father from Lithuania. As a child, "Trudy" had an insatiable desire to read and learn, and she took an interest in all subjects. It was the fact that her grandfather had died of leukaemia that fostered her interest in science. At the age of 15, she began studying chemistry at Hunter College, New York, in the hope that she might one day develop medicines to cure or prevent the disease that had claimed her grandfather.

The campus at Hunter College was for women only, so Elion was used to women studying science. However, in the world outside college, men still dominated, and despite her outstanding academic record, Elion found it impossible to get funding to take on a PhD. By doing several poorly paid jobs, she managed to save up enough money to enrol at night school, and she received a masters degree in 1941, but never received a PhD. That year, many men were out of the country fighting in the Second World War, so some laboratories were employing women. In 1944, after several years of working in unchallenging jobs in the chemical industry, Elion began work as a senior research chemist in the New York laboratory of the pharmaceuticals company Burroughs Wellcome. There she worked as an assistant to American doctor and chemist George Hitchings (1905–1998), who encouraged her to learn as much as possible and to follow her own lines of enquiry.

Although Elion had studied chemistry, her quest to produce medicines had led her to biochemistry (the chemistry of living things), pharmacology (the study of how drugs work) and virology (the study of viruses). By the 1940s, biochemists had discovered that a chemical called DNA (deoxyribonucleic acid) present in the cell nucleus was involved in cell replication. They had worked out the constituent parts of DNA, but its double helix structure would not be worked out until 1953. The most important constituents are small molecules called purines and pyrimidines, which join together in pairs along the length of the much larger DNA molecule. Elion wondered whether altering these molecules might somehow confuse a virus

LEFT: *Gertrude Elion and George Hitchings, photographed shortly after winning the Nobel Prize for Medicine, in 1988. In 1991 Elion became the first woman to be inducted into the US National Inventors Hall of Fame. Elion worked closely with Hitchings for much of her career.*

BELOW LEFT: *Replica of DNA model originally assembled by English biologist Francis Crick (1916–2004) and American molecular biologist James Watson (b. 1928) in 1953. Along the length of each helical strand are the purines and pyrimidines, the key to most of Gertrude Elion's inventions.*

BELOW: *Molecular structure of 6-mercaptopurine (6-MP), developed by Elion and Hutchings in 1951. 6-MP has a very similar shape to purine molecules found along the length of DNA, and it interrupts their formation, inhibiting the rampant reproduction of DNA characteristic of cancers.*

or a bacterium or stop the uncontrolled reproduction of cancer cells. So she and Hitchings set about engineering new ones.

Elion and Hitchings made their first breakthrough in 1948. One of their purines, 2,6-diaminopurine, was found to restrict the reproduction of bacteria, and to slow the growth of tumours in mice. Over the next few years, Elion tested more than 100 other engineered purines. In 1951, trials in rats suggested that one of them, 6-mercaptopurine (6-MP), could fight leukaemia. At the time, there was little hope for patients with leukaemia, most of whom were children and most of whom died within a few months of diagnosis. When 6-MP was tested in humans, it was found to increase life expectancy, and some children even went into full remission. The drug is still used today in anti-cancer chemotherapy.

With increasing knowledge of biochemical reactions at the heart of cell biology, Elion went on to synthesize several medicines effective against a range of bacterial diseases, including malaria, meningitis and septicaemia. In 1958, she produced the first medicine that could suppress the immune system, making organ transplants safer (see box). In 1981, after more than a decade's work, she created the first anti-viral drug, acyclovir, which is the active substance in anti-herpes medicine such as Zovirax® and Valtrex®. Gertrude Elion received many awards for her groundbreaking work in chemotherapy, including, in 1988, the Nobel Prize in Physiology or Medicine. She shared the prize with George Hitchings and Scottish pharmacologist James Black (b.1924), for "discoveries of important principles for drug treatment".

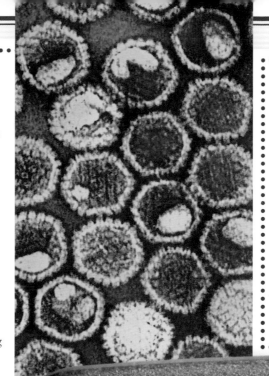

LEFT: *False-colour electron micrograph of herpes simplex viruses. Each virus comprises DNA in a protein "cage" (the capsid), surrounded by a fatty membrane (the envelope). A virus uses resources inside a host cell to reproduce; Elion produced the first effective anti-viral drugs, which inhibit this process.*

ABOVE: *Today there are dozens of anti-viral drugs available, including this one, Valtrex®. The active ingredient in this drug is a derivative of acyclovir, developed by Elion. Valtrex® is used to treat all kinds of herpes infections, including genital herpes, shingles and AIDS-related herpes.*

BELOW: *Surgeons removing and preparing a human kidney in preparation for transplantation into a recipient. Since the development of immunosuppressive drugs — such as azathioprine, developed by Elion — there is no need for the donor and recipient to be related to avoid rejection of the organ by the recipient's body.*

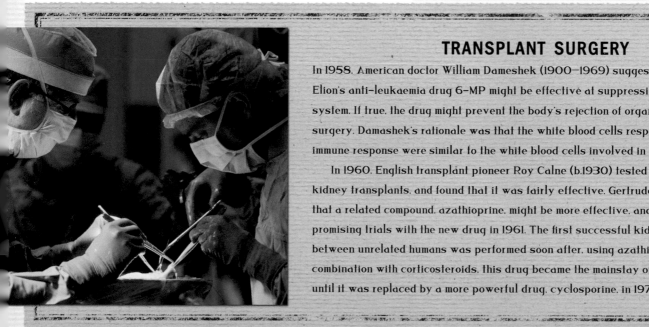

TRANSPLANT SURGERY

In 1958, American doctor William Dameshek (1900–1969) suggested that Gertrude Elion's anti-leukaemia drug 6-MP might be effective at suppressing the immune system. If true, the drug might prevent the body's rejection of organs after transplant surgery. Dameshek's rationale was that the white blood cells responsible for the immune response were similar to the white blood cells involved in leukaemia.

In 1960, English transplant pioneer Roy Calne (b.1930) tested 6-MP in dog kidney transplants, and found that it was fairly effective. Gertrude Elion suggested that a related compound, azathioprine, might be more effective, and Calne conducted promising trials with the new drug in 1961. The first successful kidney transplant between unrelated humans was performed soon after, using azathioprine. In combination with corticosteroids, this drug became the mainstay of transplant surgery, until it was replaced by a more powerful drug, cyclosporine, in 1978.

TIM BERNERS-LEE

(BORN 8 JUNE 1955)

I**N MODERN LIFE, IT SEEMS INCREASINGLY HARD FOR AN INDIVIDUAL TO INVENT SOMETHING THAT TRULY CHANGES THE WORLD. HOWEVER, ONE PERSON WHO DID JUST THAT IS ENGLISH PHYSICIST AND COMPUTER SCIENTIST TIM BERNERS-LEE. IN 1990, HE LAUNCHED THE WORLD WIDE WEB.**

Timothy Berners-Lee was born in London. His parents were both computer scientists. As a boy, Tim became interested in electronics after building circuits to control his model train set. He studied physics at Oxford University; while he was there, he built his first computer. After graduating in 1976, he worked as a computer systems engineer at various companies.

In 1980, Berners-Lee spent six months at the European Organization for Nuclear Research, a particle physics facility in the outskirts of Geneva, on the border between France and Switzerland. It is better known by the acronym CERN, which derives from the facility's original name, Conseil Européen pour la Recherche Nucléaire. While at CERN, Berners-Lee devised a computer system, for his own personal use, to store and retrieve information. Named ENQUIRE, this was a forerunner of the Web. It was based upon hyperlinks, cross-references in one document that enable a computer to call up another, related document.

In 1984, Berners-Lee was back at CERN, on a computing fellowship programme. He became frustrated by the lack of compatibility between different computer systems, and between documents written using different software applications. In a memo he sent to his manager in 1989, Berners-Lee set out his vision of a "universal linked information system" with which to organize the huge amounts of information produced at CERN. He proposed that a "web of links" would be more useful than the "fixed, hierarchical system" that existed. Documents available on computers within CERN's network would contain hyperlinks to other documents, including those on different computers. In 1990, Berners-Lee's manager encouraged him to spend some time – as a side project – on developing his idea.

During the autumn of 1990, Berners-Lee, along with his colleague, Belgian computer scientist Robert Cailliau (b.1947), created all the now-familiar fundamental components of the World Wide Web. The universal language he invented

Right: *A 1994 screenshot of the first web browser, World Wide Web. Berners-Lee wrote the software exclusively for NEXT computers, like the one he used at CERN. The software could read and edit pages written in html, open linked pages and download any linked computer files.*

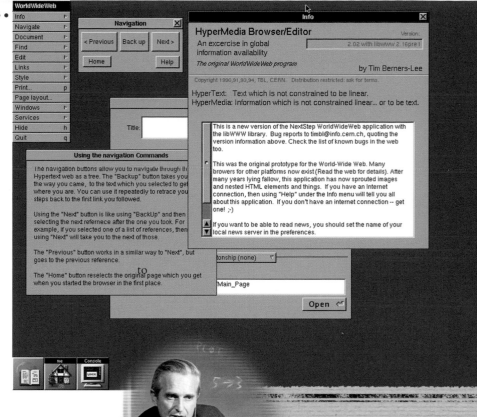

for writing linked documents (web pages) is "html" – hypertext markup language. The software that responds to "requests" from hyperlinks is called a "web server", a term that also refers the hardware that hosts the web pages. And the language, or protocol, computers use to communicate the hyperlink requests is "http" – hypertext transfer protocol. Berners-Lee had to write the first web browser, the application used to view the documents hosted on web servers. He called his browser "WorldWideWeb". Berners-Lee also wrote the first web pages, which he published on his server in December 1990. It was on 25th of that month that Berners-Lee first "surfed" from one web page to another, via http, by clicking a hyperlink in his browser.

The following year, Berners-Lee made available his software to people outside CERN, and the idea quickly caught on. By 1994, the Web had grown so much that each "resource" – a document or image, for example – needed a unique "address" on the Internet. In consultation with the Web community, Berners-Lee created the format for web addresses, called the "uniform resource locator" (URL). After 1994, the Web spread rapidly beyond academic and military circles. Within a few short years, most people in the world had been affected directly by its existence, and millions were already regularly "surfing" from document to document online.

Tim Berners-Lee has received a huge number of accolades for his invention, which he gave free to the world without patents or rights. In 1994, he founded the World Wide Web Consortium, which helps keep the Web working smoothly and aims to foster its future growth. He also campaigns to keep the Internet "neutral" – free of restrictions on content and what kinds of computers may be connected.

WHERE THE WEB WAS BORN

Left: *A plaque at CERN commemorating the invention of the Web.*

DOUG ENGELBART (1925–)

Two very important technologies underpinned Tim Berners-Lee's invention of the World Wide Web: hyperlinks and the computer mouse. American computer scientist Douglas Engelbart invented the mouse in 1967, and he was also heavily involved in the development of hyperlinks.

In the 1960s, Engelbart headed a team at the Augmentation Research Center, at the Stanford Research Institute, California. Engelbart's team devised an online "collaboration system" called NLS (oN-Line System). This included the first use of hyperlinks and the mouse, which Engelbart invented in 1967. In 1968, Engelbart demonstrated NLS to a large audience of computer scientists. In addition to hyperlinks and the mouse, the 90–minute session, normally referred to as "The Mother of All Demos", introduced such ideas as e–mail, video–conferencing and real–time collaboration between computer users far apart.

INDEX

Page numbers in *italics* refer to picture captions.